The Eye Opening

The Eye Opening

enlightenment is possible

by Michael LoPatriello

Independently published

ISBN: 9781705538142

Cover art by Heather Pratt, instagram: @hprattart

Dedicated to my mother
Thank you for encouraging me to write this book,
and to follow my heart.
Thank you for being one of the few people that have ever really understood me.

Contents

Introduction: an Attempt at the Ineffable ix

PART 1: I OPEN, THE EYE OPENS 1

- The Heart Opens, the Search Begins 3
- A Snake in the Desert 7
- Spiraling Serpent 14
- The Third Eye 21
- The Nightmare 40
- Ubiquitous Rites of Passage 46
- The Pursuit of Enlightenment 51
  - BE PASSIONATE 53
  - SURRENDER 54
  - BREATHE DEEPLY 56
  - EXPLORE YOGA 58
  - READ SPIRITUAL ENCOURAGEMENT FROM MASTERS 60
- Enough… Rise 61

PART 2: 9 SPIRITUAL TRUTHS 67

- 1: The One is the All, the All are the One 69
- 2: The Golden Rule 76
- 3: Know Thyself 80
- 4: Creator is in your Heart 88
- 5: Become like a Child 94
- 6: Surrender 97
- 7: Silence: the Truth is Beyond Logic and Language 103
- 8: Reality is a Dream we Create 108
- 9: The One in Everything is Love 113

Contact 123

Sources & Permissions 125

Introduction: an Attempt at the Ineffable

"We are a species with amnesia."
–Graham Hancock

When I was 20 years old, while sobbing in a park in Prague, Czech Republic, an eye of vibrating energy suddenly opened in the center of my head and revealed to me love-light glistening and radiating from myself and from every single thing around me.

This brief experience forever changed my life. It felt like an orgasm but in the middle of my brain. It felt as if I had entered heaven, paradise, our true home. Earth was glowing with a loving presence that was not separate from my true identity.

I believe I experienced what has been called the third eye. I believe it was a momentary glimpse of human's profound, forgotten potential.

Such awakenings, revelations, and epiphanies cannot be truly explained in words. They are very personal. They are intimate moments of the soul opening up to its true nature. One must have the experience to understand.

So why write a book? Why attempt to share in words that which is indescribable? The attempt is worth it because such experiences serve as a reminder. We have forgotten the truth, and the truth is exciting and worth my feeble attempt to put it into words.

What is the truth? The truth is that everything is in fact One. The individual is the same identity, deep down, as everything else. We are all One energy, One life, One consciousness, One intelligence, One love. Realizing and experiencing this in every moment is enlightenment, and enlightenment leads to ultimate happiness.

This has been proclaimed repeatedly throughout history by masters, mystics, saints, and yogis. This can be, and has been, heard a thousand times without bringing any sort of change in an individual's life. It will not hit home or change anything until the oneness of life is experienced firsthand, within the individual's own consciousness and heart.

Ever since my momentary glimpse of the One love-light in all things and my intimate connection to it, I have wanted others to see and feel it too, because such moments are life-changing, and what humanity needs is a change. The change must start individually, on the personal level. It starts with you. Feeling and perceiving your own deep unity with the universe changes your motivation, your mindset, your state of being…everything! It changes everything. Fear vanishes. You realize that love is what you are and what everything fundamentally is and has always been. You remember that you are taken care of, are eternal, are pure energy, pure light, and are a co-creator in this beautiful, mysterious, infinite, dreamlike universe.

Direct experience is crucial. The world now is saturated with information. This is fantastic because data once impossible to obtain can be found by anyone with internet access.

Knowledge is power, but true knowing does not come from more information. It comes from experience. However, information can help lead us to an experience. Spiritual wisdom and testimonies of awakening can remind us of what is possible and of what we are capable of, and therefore, can inspire us to push beyond our limiting beliefs and strive for a direct experience for ourselves. They can point the way back to the house of true knowing, to the sacred space of silence beyond thinking, to the space within the heart.

I hope this personal account of illumination does just that.

There is much, much more to us than what we have been taught and led to believe. I have only scratched the surface. Today's paradigm is blind to what we really are and are capable of. Our identity, the universe's source-energy, is mysterious and fantastic. I have had but a few peeks into it, and every time, so brilliant was its light, so overwhelming its grace, I swooned.

This book is about a profound, spiritual experience I had, the path that led me to it, and the wisdom discovered along the way. I hope it inspires you to strive for your own awakening and encourages you to keep striving until you achieve one. At the very least I hope it gives you pause to reconsider what you truly are.

In Part 1 I attempt the ineffable and tell my story. All I ask is for you to try to keep an open mind. Only then do you keep an open heart.

In Part 2 I share 9 main spiritual truths that are found in the majority of the world's religious, spiritual, and channeled texts. There are many voices, but one Self. Cut through the dogma, the drama, the metaphors, and the cultural differences, and one finds that most spiritual writings share these fundamental themes.

These 9 resonate with my personal, spiritual experiences. The accompanying quotes have aided me greatly in my quest for alignment with the universe. I hope they may help you as well.

Thank you for reading and thank you for seeking.

(A few of the following chapters begin with a poem. These are written by me, unless noted otherwise, and are from my book: *Attempt at the Ineffable: poems, rants, short stories, and a play*.)

PART 1:

I OPEN, THE EYE OPENS

"The most beautiful thing we can experience is the mysterious. It is the source of all true art and science. He to whom the emotion is a stranger, who can no longer pause to wonder and stand wrapped in awe, is as good as dead; his eyes are closed."
–Albert Einstein

"I saw that the universe is not comprised of dead matter, but is on the contrary, a living presence; I became conscious within myself of eternal life … I saw that everyone is immortal; that the cosmic order is such that … all things work together for the good of each and all; that the foundation principle of the world, of all the worlds, is what we call love, and that happiness of each and all is in the long run absolutely certain."
–R.M. Bucke, *Cosmic Consciousness*

The Heart Opens, the Search Begins

"Let those who seek, continue to seek until they find."
–Jesus, Gospel of Thomas

For most of my life I have not felt fully myself in interactions. In almost every encounter, with the few exceptions of close family members and loved ones, it is like I suddenly become a character that I automatically perform. Always afterwards, I feel I must shake off the performance. I look back in bewilderment at the act I just put on. Was that me? Why did I act that way? This was particularly strong in my younger years. I felt like the other's perception of me would dictate how I would perform in our interaction, and I would, without thinking, pick up their cue and play along. This was confusing and awkward.

"Is it their perception that causes me to take on a role and become a character? Am I the cause of this constant changing of masks? Why does this happen subconsciously, automatically, and without effort? If I change from each perception of me, in each encounter, then who am I? I keep changing characters. It feels like I am none of them, or am I all of them? Who is the wearer of these costumes and masks?" I was very chameleonic. This led me to deeply question: who am I?

Arguably this is the most important question in life. This is the starting point for all spiritual searching. What are we really? What is consciousness? Is it just a product of chemical reactions in the brain? Are we just a body? Merely physical? Are we our thoughts and feelings alone? Who is aware of the feelings? Who is observing the thoughts? Who is the thinker that does the thinking but who cannot be thought?

What am I? This question has always been there, deep within. It planted a seed early on that would later grow into motivation to fully engage in an all-out search for truth.

To add even more mystery to my identity, I began having what I now call heart openings.

During around the time I was in junior high, I started having episodes of intense emotional release. I still have them occasionally, but not as often as I did then. Some would say they were panic attacks. Others would call them emotional breakdowns. For me they were and are a great deal more than that.

These episodes happen sporadically and infrequently, but they all share the same progression. First, I grow anxious. Sometimes they are induced by excitement, but more often than not it is anxiety and stress.

The panic rises, and I feel a pain in my chest begin to grow. The sensation is as if my heart tightens and cramps. My mind races and I begin to mentally freak out. A worry builds upon another worry, and I scramble to make sense of what is happening. Everything accelerates: the pain in my heart, the race in my mind, and the overall uncertainty. I have heard that panic attacks have similar symptoms of a heart attack, and I can relate. The attack becomes a whirlwind of panic, a tightening of my heart and chest, a growing sense of impending doom, and it becomes too much to bear. Becoming overwhelmed, I eventually let go to the rising emotion.

I surrender. I begin to sob. Deep and quick breaths ensue, full and rapid inhales and exhales that completely fill then empty my lungs. I cry hard, like an infant. The pressure and pain in my chest subside and it feels as if my heart suddenly opens.

Then a warm and loving presence pours out from my heart and fills my body. Its trembling and potent energy overcomes me, and I feel its intelligence. My once crazed mind is hushed with a soothing, peaceful, omnipotent silence. I continue to sob, and I feel like a small child again. In these moments, I know I am taken care of, and loved. There are no questions, no worries, but a deep wisdom and acknowledgment of my Source, of what feels like home and my true abiding place.

These moments stand out. Nothing else compares to them. They are unique and magnificent. Others that have been around me during such episodes think I am sad, or think something is wrong, or judge and feel uncomfortable from the intensity of my sobs. I am not sad, far from it. I am overwhelmed by an indescribable love and energy that blossoms from within my heart. No other experience has come close to these episodes of my heart opening, apart from my third eye experience, which I go into depth in a later chapter.

When my mind seems to be going off the rails, taking on more than it is designed to take on, worrying about and trying to control things that it should not and cannot, it's as if a loving, bigger, wiser presence knocks at my heart and asks to come in and help. There is no room for it while my mind freaks out, stomps around, and throws a tantrum. Only when I let go, drop all mental effort, and surrender, does the space clear and allow room for the love energy from the heart to enter. Its motherly presence comes rushing in and embraces the frightened child who once thought he was all alone.

These openings, along with my constant questioning of who I really was, and a growing uneasiness of what society expected of me as a soon-to-be-adult, led me to change my path and seek for answers. Throughout high school my suspicion grew stronger that my true identity and the true identity of everyone was much more than what society believed. Nothing in school could explain my heart experiences. So, I started my search. I yearned for truth, for something real. Everything I was being taught felt fake, felt like just half-truths, not the whole story. I dropped the path laid out for me of a prestigious college and lucrative career and I went looking.

I left high school after my first semester of senior year and traveled alone to India. I had enough credits to graduate early. India to me represented the land of enlightened masters and awakened yogis, a place where I could find some answers. I wandered through small villages in the foothills of the Himalayas. I began to feel lost. I was naïve. I was innocent. I was not finding what I was expecting to find. When I was really losing hope and feeling like a failure, I befriended a local who brought me to a meditation center and entered me into a ten-day course of silent meditation.

I was wandering around looking for some master, and then it was as if the universe sat me down and said, "Be still. Be silent. Listen. Your master is within you." My trip to India was intense and sobering, but it taught me an important lesson: what I was looking for is within.

After I returned home, I applied to and attended Naropa University, a Buddhist school in Boulder, Colorado. During my studies there, I also did my own research. I read books of religion, mystical poetry, theosophy, metaphysics, mythology, and spirituality. I noticed that, at their foundation, all religions and spiritual belief systems were saying the same things. I discovered 9 main spiritual truths. One of these drove home what I had already learned during my travels in India: know thyself, because you are that which you seek. The consciousness in the individual is one with the consciousness that created everything. Therefore, why look anywhere else for the answers other than within?

So, I began looking within myself for the answers. I was passionate in my search. Nothing else mattered. I was anti-social and awkward in my first few years in college and was constantly self-reflecting. Most of my time was spent alone in nature writing or with my face buried in books.

In those books I found symbology that reminded me of two visions I had at a younger age. The newfound connection only threw more fuel on the fire of my burning curiosity and amazement. The imagery was of snakes and would eventually lead me to explore Yoga.

A Snake in the Desert

> "The serpent shows the way to hidden things..."
> –Carl G. Jung

My first vision occurred at some point during my early high school years. I received it in a dream. I call it a vision because it was more than just a dream. It evoked an intense emotion and had a distinct clarity and intriguing imagery. Unlike most dreams I have, I still clearly remember it today. I believe it contained an important message.

I was on my knees in a desert. It was twilight and all I could see were sand dunes and the sky speckled with faint stars.

In front of me, out of the sand, suddenly arose my twin sister. She carried a large snake, resembling a boa constrictor. It draped over her arms and shoulders. Her presence was angelic. She was glowing with a golden light. The sight of her was powerful. Her eyes shined, and she looked wise and peaceful, with a gentle smile. I could feel a loving energy radiating from her. Her presence was so overwhelming that I began to weep.

She arose out of the sand and continued upwards. As she and the snake rose higher and higher up into the sky, with sand still cascading from her shoulders and the snake's body, they began to shine brighter and brighter, until I could not see them, only the bright light. Then I woke up.

At that time, I did not know the significance of snakes used as symbols. It was only later, while doing my own research in college, that I realized their prevalence in spirituality.

What I found astounded me. Snake worship and snake symbolism were commonplace in almost all the ancient cultures around the world.

> "Ophiolatreia, the worship of the serpent … is one of the most remarkable … forms of religion the world has ever known. There is hardly a country of the ancient world where it cannot be traced, pervading every known system of mythology … Babylon, Persia, Hinduostan, Ceylon, China, Japan, Burma, Java, Arabia, Syria, Asia, Minor, Egypt, Ethiopia, Greece, Italy, Northern and Western Europe, Mexico, Peru, and America."
> –Hargrave Jennings, *Ophiolatreia*

> "All of the Logoi of all the ancient religious systems are connected with, and symbolized by, serpents."
> –H.P. Blavatsky, *The Secret Doctrine*

> "Serpent worship in some form has permeated nearly all parts of the earth. The serpent mounds of the American Indians; Python, the great snake of the Greeks; the sacred serpents of the Druids; the Midgard snake of Scandinavia; the Nagas of Burma, Siam, and Cambodia; the brazen serpent of the Jews; the mystic serpent of Orpheus; the snakes at the Oracle of Delphi twining themselves around the tripod upon which the Pythian priestess sat, the tripod itself being in the form of twisted serpents; the sacred serpents preserved in the Egyptian temples; the Uraeus coiled upon the foreheads of the pharaohs and priests; –all these bear witness to the universal veneration in which the snake was held."
> –Manly P. Hall, *The Secret Teachings of All Ages*

> "The serpent is a symbol found everywhere in the Greek archaic religious record as well as the Egyptian. The depiction of the snake refers to 'earth energy' or, in the words of John Chang, 'yin power' (yin chi rising from the earth). Certain researchers have purposed the theory that the chakras of Eastern mysticism are no more than a network of 'standing waves' in the field of

yin energy that surrounds and pervades us. … All the images [of a snake coiling up] refer to the ascension of earth energy."
–Kosta Danaos, *The Magus of Java*[1]

Investigating snake imagery further, I came across Yoga and Kundalini. At the time I only knew Yoga as most westerners do: as a sequence of stretches and held body positions. I quickly realized that Yoga was an ancient method for attaining enlightenment.

Within the Yogic belief system, Kundalini refers to the primal energy of creation, located in the body at the bottom of the spine. It is symbolized by a coiled snake. When activated it travels up the spine through the body's energy centers or chakras. Not only does it lie dormant in the human body but is also considered the Goddess and energy of all manifested creation.

"Kundalini represents the cosmic vital energy lying dormant in the human body which is coiled round the base of the spine, a little below the sexual organ, like a serpent fast asleep and closing with her mouth the aperture of the sushumna, the hairlike duct rising through the center of the spinal cord to the conscious center at the top of the head. When aroused, Kundalini, they said, rises through the sushumna like a streak of lightning, carrying with her the vital energy of the body, which for the time being becomes cold and lifeless, with complete or partial cessation of vital functions, to join her divine spouse Shiva in the last or seventh center in the brain. In the course of this process, the embodied self, freed from the bondage of flesh, passed into a condition of ecstasy known as samadhi, realizing itself as deathless, full of bliss, and one with the all-pervading Supreme Consciousness."
–Gopi Krishna, *Living with Kundalini: The autobiography of Gopi Krishna*[2]

---

[1] *The Magus of Java* by Kosta Danaos published by Inner Traditions International and Bear & Company, ©2000. All rights reserved. http://www.Innertraditions.com Reprinted with permission of publisher.

[2] From *Living with Kundalini: The Autobiography of Gopi Krishna*, by Gopi Krishna, © 1967, 1970 by James Hillman. Reprinted by arrangement with The Permissions Company, LLC,

"Kundalini… the figure of a coiled female serpent—a serpent goddess not of 'gross' but of 'subtle' substance—which is to be thought of as residing in a torpid, slumbering state in a subtle center, the first of the seven, near the base of the spine: the aim of the Yoga then being to rouse this serpent, lift her head, and bring her up a subtle nerve or channel of the spine to the so-called 'thousand-petaled lotus' (sahasrara) at the crown of the head. … she, rising from the lowest to the highest lotus center, will pass through and wake the five between, and with each wakening the psychology and personality of the practitioner will be altogether and fundamentally transformed."
–Joseph Campbell, *The Mythic Image*

"The most important concept to grasp about the energy field is that the lower or negative pole will draw the universal energy into itself from the cosmos. From there it will move upward to be met and reacted to by the positive spiraling energy moving downward from within. The measure of an entity's level of ray activity is the locus wherein the south pole outer energy has been met by the inner spiraling positive energy. As an entity grows more polarized this locus will move upwards. This phenomenon has been called by your peoples the Kundalini. However, it may better be thought of as the meeting place of cosmic and inner, shall we say, vibratory understanding."
–The Law of One, Book 2

I could not deny the connection between my vision and the imagery of Kundalini: the snake, the light, the rising, and the profound feeling of divinity my sister exuded.

The vision also shares a similarity with an image Jesus speaks of in the bible:

---

on behalf of Shambhala Publications, Inc., Boulder, Colorado, https://www.shambhala.com/

> "And as Moses lifted up the serpent in the wilderness, so must the Son of man be lifted up."
> –Jesus, John 3:14, *The Holy Bible King James Version*

My twin sister was literally lifting a serpent out of the wilderness. The Judaean desert that Jesus fasted in for forty days and forty nights after his baptism is referred to as the wilderness.

> "Then Jesus was led by the Spirit into the wilderness to be tempted..."
> –Matthew 4:1, *The Holy Bible New International Version*

The snake imagery was already within me. It was in my consciousness. I did not know about Kundalini, Ophiolatreia (the worship of serpents), or the prominent use of snakes in myths and spiritual symbols all over the globe.

The fact that it was my twin sister is relevant to Kundalini.

Kundalini's main goal of spiritual awakening is reached by joining the universal male and female energies within the body. In Yoga ideology, the human body has three main channels, called nadis, that energy uses to travel up the spine: ida, pingala, and sushumna. The sushumna rises through the center of the spine, while the other two are on left and right of it. Ida, originating on the left, is associated with lunar energy, the feminine, and the goddess Shakti. Pingala, on the right, is associated with solar energy, the masculine, and the god Shiva.

> "The purpose of Kundalini Yoga is to reunite Shiva and Shakti, to create the eternal form of Shiva, Sadashiva. Sadashiva's left side is female and the right side is male; the two principals have united but have not yet merged. If they were to merge that would be the end of the play. … Sadashiva exists on the cosmic scale; in an individual this deity is called Ardhanarishvara ('the Lord Who is Half Female'). In order to manifest Sadashiva the Kundalini must be made to rise fully, because the highest manifestation of Shiva in the human being is in the head, the highest part of the body."
> –Robert E. Svoboda, *Aghora II: Kundalini*

> "Shakti [feminine power] and Shiva [masculine power] become one and in their union, everything... gets dissolved. Further, there is nothing more to experience beyond [this]. Hence let me stop speaking of it. For it is useless to talk."
> –*Dnyaneshwari*, lines 306-318

> "The object is to awaken Kundalini through ritual practices and to enable her ascent up the sushumna nadi through the chakra system. When it reaches the topmost chakra the blissful union of Shiva and Shakti occurs. This leads to a far-reaching transformation of the personality."
> –Sonu Shamdasani, in C.G. Jung's *The Psychology of Kundalini Yoga*

> "In the evolution of the yogin there is always the union of both the man and woman powers."
> –Wilhelm Hauer, in C.G. Jung's *The Psychology of Kundalini Yoga*

Shiva and Shakti, or the pingala and the ida, seem to represent not only the opposite sexes, but the opposite expressions of everything, the polarity and duality in all of manifestation: ying and yang, Father Sky and Mother Earth, hot and cold, day and night, sun and moon, etc.

Hatha Yoga, today in the west, is thought of as a stretching sequence, but originally had to do with the joining of these two energies. "Ha" means the sun, and "Tha" means the moon. It is an ancient approach of Yoga that starts with the body, its energy centers, and the cleansing of the system to allow the two polar energies to flow together and rise up the spine. Whereas Ashtanga Yoga, based on Patanjali's Yoga Sutras, starts with the 8 limbs of Yoga, and focuses on moral and self-conduct. The bringing together, balancing, and unification of these two cosmic forces within the body, the Ha and the Tha, solar and lunar energies, leads to awakened powers and perceptions.

> "If two make peace with one another in this one house, they will say to the mountain: Be removed, and it will be removed."
> –Jesus, Gospel of Thomas, *The Nag Hammadi Library*

It seemed the universe was leading me to Yoga and its mysterious Kundalini, because my second vision with similar snake imagery had an even more obvious connection to it.

Spiraling Serpent

kunda-free-me

my center line
my spine
my axis of symmetry
seems to be a seam
within lies infinity
fold after fold
ceaselessly expanding
an ever-changing mold
and opening further and further within
I spin

My second vision occurred in Cancun, Mexico, on a family vacation during my high school years. This one was not a dream. It arose during one of my heart openings. Up until this point of my life I had had other heart opening experiences, as described earlier. They are all similar to that description. So, it was not my first, but this one was unique because of an accompanying vision.

I was sitting with my mother and brother on the floor in the living room of the beach house we had rented for the week. We were allowing my brother to express his feelings about our parents' recent divorce. He was upset with our mom, so we were talking about it and working things out.

I remember looking at my brother, listening to his anger, and feeling love for him and for my mother. There was a building pressure in my heart, like my previous heart openings. My mom asked if there was anything I wanted to say to my brother. All I said was, "I love you."

At some point I began to cry, and then sob. It was deep, rapid, convulsive breathing, like an infant. My mind was quiet, and the pressure in my heart eased and it felt like a dam fell and warm water rushed forth from my heart to the rest of my body. My face began to buzz and vibrate with a tangible energy. All very similar to my past experiences, but then came an image.

I saw myself suspended in a vast, empty, black space. I was floating and slowly rising. Around me was a giant snake, spiraling upwards with his giant head way above me. Above his head was a bright shining light, so bright it obscured the view of his head and face, as if I were looking up at a thin cloud that was in front of the sun. I was floating slowly upwards towards the head and light, in the center of the spiral that the snake's huge body formed.

The image was exactly like the Rod of Asclepius symbol, but no rod, and resembled Hermes' Caduceus, but only one snake. I was moving along the line that the rod makes in both symbols. I suddenly heard a warning as I looked up towards the light. "Be careful, that is where the head is." And the vision ended.

The buzzing energy slowly subsided, as did my tears. I relaxed in bliss; the release always felt so supremely divine, and I was grateful that it had happened. It had not for a long time.

More snakes. This time the relation to Kundalini was more obvious. The snake was spiraling up towards a light and the light was just above the snake's head, just as so many drawings of Kundalini depict.

In the vision with my sister, I also was crying, and was also overcome with emotion. This time it was more tangible because I was awake and more aware of my body. The heart felt wide open, and the energy rising from it to my face was remarkably strong. The heart felt almost like a heating lamp, giving off loving light and warmth. It felt amazing.

In Yoga, the heart is the fourth chakra, called anahata.

> "The elevation of the human will to aims transcendent of this bestial order of life requires, according to the yogic model, an awakening that will not be of the pelvic region, but of chakra 4, which is of the heart. The name of this transformative center, anahata, has the curious meaning, 'not hit,' which is interpreted as signifying 'the Sound that is not made by any two things striking together.' For every sound heard by the physical ear is of things rubbing or striking together. That of the voice, for example, is of breath on the vocal chords. The one sound not so made is the great tone, or hum (sabda), of the creative energy (maya, shakti) of which things are the manifestations, or epiphanies. And the intuitive recognition of this creative tone within a phenomenal form is what opens the heart to love. What before had been an 'it' becomes then a 'thou,' alive with the tone of creation... an awakening (metaphorically) to a New World (the Promised Land) and to Life in the Spirit (the Virgin Birth)."
> –Joseph Campbell, *The Inner Reaches of Outer Space*[3]

The awakening of anahata is the awakening of love for the life in all things. Manifested diversity is transformed and unified by the heart's recognition and love.

> "Indha (i.e. the Kindler) by name is this person here in the right eye ... Now that which has the form of a person in the left eye is his wife, Virāj. Their meeting-place is the space in the heart. Their food is the red lump in the heart. Their covering is the net-like work in the heart. The path that they go is that vein which goes upward from the heart."

–Brihadaranyaka Upanishad 4.2.2, *The Thirteen Principal Upanishads* trans. Robert Ernest Hume

Again, we see mention of the masculine and feminine. Here their union is said to take place in the heart, after which they travel up towards the head. The opening of the heart center has always been the initiator of all my spiritual experiences. The heart's importance is one of the 9 truths that I found in my research. It is a main theme that comes up again and again in religious and spiritual texts. Simply put, it is the location of the Creator within the individual. It is our source of life in the body, and our spiritual source, the Source of all life.

Another symbol, other than Kundalini spiraling up the spine to the head, which closely resembles the snake in this vision, is the Rod of Asclepius from Greek mythology as I mentioned before. A single snake wraps up and around a rod held by the Greek god Asclepius, who is associated with medicine and healing. This is like Moses' pole in the Bible:

> "And the Lord said unto Moses, Make thee a fiery serpent, and set it upon a pole: and it shall come to pass, that every one that is bitten, when he looketh upon it, shall live. And Moses made a serpent of brass, and put it upon a pole, and it came to pass, that if a serpent had bitten any man, when he beheld the serpent of brass, he lived."
> –Numbers 21:8-9, *The Holy Bible King James Version*

In the vision, I was suspended and rising towards the head and the light. Relating back to Kundalini, it was like I was in the sushumna rising in the center, toward the sahasrara, the last chakra located at the top of the head.

> "We must all ascend to the heights, the very highest in consciousness to receive our illumination. This height means the very top of the head and there, if the faculty is not developed, we must develop it with spiritual thoughts. Then from the heart, the love center, we must let love flow forth to balance all and when this is done the Christ is revealed."

–Baird T. Spalding, *Life and Teaching of the Masters of the Far East V.1*

"The center at the top of the head is the highest focus in the human body, and there the Silver Cord of 'Liquid White Light' from the Great Source of Creation enters."
–Godfre Ray King, *Unveiled Mysteries*

"In the course of Her [Kundalini's] ascent from Her seat at the base of the spine to the crown, it is averred that She waters with nectar the six lotuses flourishing at the six important nerve junctions on the cerebrospinal axis governing the vital and sensory organs, which bloom at Her approach, until She arrives at the thousand-petalled lotus at the top of the head and is absorbed in ecstatic union with Her heavenly consort. When released from the chains which bind it to earth, the embodied consciousness soars to sublime heights of self-realization, made aware for the first time after ages of bondage of its own ineffable, deathless nature."
–Gopi Krishna, *Living with Kundalini: The autobiography of Gopi Krishna*

"Piercing the head at the point where is the edge of the hair … He obtains self-rule. He obtains the lord of the mind, lord of the voice, lord of the eye, lord of the ear, lord of the understanding—this and more he becomes, even Brahma, whose body is space, whose soul is the real, whose pleasure-ground is the breathing spirit, whose mind is bliss, abounding in tranquility, immortal. —Thus, O Prācīnayogya (Man of the Ancient Yoga), worship."
–Taittiriya Upanishad 1.6.1-2, *The Thirteen Principal Upanishads* trans. Robert Ernest Hume

"It comes to us from the Universal through the Christ within, which has already been born within us all. As a minute speck it enters through the Christ, or super conscious mind, the place of

> receptivity within ourselves. Then it must be carried to the mount or highest within ourselves, the very top of the head. It is held there. We must then allow the Holy Spirit to descend."
> –Baird T. Spalding, *Life and Teaching of the Masters of the Far East V.1*

The Native American tribe of the Hopi shares an exact description of Kundalini process:

> "Man is created perfect in the image of his Creator. Then after closing the door (at the top of the head) and falling from grace into the uninhibited expression of his own human will, he begins the slow climb upward. … With this turn man rises upward, bringing into predominant function each of the higher centers. The door at the crown of the head then opens, and he merges into wholeness of all Creation, whence he sprang."
> –Frank Waters, *Book of the Hopi*

As I rose and gazed up towards the head of the snake and the light, I heard the warning, "Be careful, that is where the head is." I pondered the meaning of this for several years. Yes, that is where the head is, meaning the light and the snake's head are where my head and brain are, but why the tone of caution?

Turns out that this was a warning for a traumatic experience that I had several years later. (Discussed in the chapter The Nightmare)

I stumbled upon snake imagery during my research, which led me to remember my visions and realize their symbolic significance, which led me to find and explore Yoga and its Kundalini. Something within me, my subconscious, the True Self, Spirit, Creator, my inner voice, whatever you wish to call it, was pointing me towards Kundalini and Yoga's ancient method of attaining enlightenment.

It was as if I asked the universe whether enlightenment was possible and if so how to attain it, and the universe replied, "Yes, it is. Check out Yoga."

I am grateful for the clues and messages received from my visions and from my research. I became more and more fascinated with mysterious

Kundalini, with my own identity, and with the subtle truth behind the physical universe.

I continued my reading of religious, spiritual, and channeled texts in search for more connections and hints. In the spring semester of my freshman year in college, I studied abroad in Prague, Czech Republic. It was here where I had my most profound experience. It was here where my third eye suddenly opened.

The Third Eye

"If the doors of perception were cleansed everything would appear to man as it is, Infinite."
–William Blake, *The Marriage of Heaven and Hell*

Star Maker's Crown

The king cracked his crown
And ever since has heard a sound
That blocks out all tranquil delight
It banters all through the night
It complains and rants about this and that
Until the king was fed up and down he sat
On a boulder by a stream
With an oak blocking the sun beam
"Enough," he cried, "Please oh please no more.
"Why do my thoughts rattle and roar?
"Cease! I demand it! Stop the chatter!"
But when the king demanded, the sound grew madder
It started up a band, a horrendous cacophony
And came to a roar with all the argument of society
The king sighed deeply with a tear in his eye
And looked down at his hands and started to cry
The entire ruckus went hush in an instant
When the king hunched over and sobbed like an infant
The band and argument all ended their violence

They recognized the truth and bowed to the silence
The king felt a warmth in his heart and heard now one sound
It was the crown on his head, ringing, re-found

Petrin Hill stands near the banks of Vltava River, and overlooks Prague. One spring afternoon I was walking up it while speaking on the phone with my mother. It was a steep cobblestone street and the trees lining it were all in bloom. Prague is especially gorgeous in spring.

I do not remember the exact conversation we were having, but the topic was spirituality and I remember being extremely excited. All I recall was that I was telling my mother about this idea I wrote down the day before in my journal. At this point I had come to a small park and was walking through it on the grass among the flowering trees of white, red, and pink. The last thing I said to her was something like, "The bigger cycle of earth is coming to spring in the galaxy. It's the springtime of the cosmos."

Suddenly, I felt my chest heave and a pressure in my heart. Initially it was like all my previous heart openings. I started to sob like a small child and the pressure released. The sobbing was rapid and deep. My mother asked what was wrong. I could not answer because I was crying so hard, so she told me to sit down somewhere. I lied down underneath a tree in the small park. I continued to sob like an infant, and as I did, I felt a warm tingling and buzzing energy rise from my left foot and left hand through my leg and arm to my heart, then from my heart up through my neck to my head and face.

The sensations and experience I had next are indescribable. What follows are words that do not come close to what I felt and saw in that moment.

The energy rising in my body reached the middle of my head and I blinked. As I blinked my eyes, my entire forehead felt like it opened and closed, felt like it blinked, and as it did my whole body shook. It felt like a big eye was suddenly in my forehead, and its opening was overwhelming. I continued to blink my eyes, and every time the forehead eye would blink in tandem, and every time I shuttered with the immensity of power, love, light, and energy that coursed through me. It felt like an orgasm in the center of my head, and I quietly gasped and moaned through my tears.

The feeling that came with it was love love love love love. Profound, deep love. A love I had never felt before. An all-consuming love. An indescribable love flowed through me, embraced me. It felt like I was picked up by a cosmic mother, and she soothed me and lulled me and said, "Shhh, hush my child. All is well. I am here."

A grand presence filled me and looked out through me. A wider perspective, a wiser, quieter, divine presence was in me and behind me and seemed to peer through me. It was not foreign, but familiar, and truer than anything else I had experienced. It felt more real as an identity than the persona and character I had played all my life. I felt like a child, and this presence was the mother, the father, not separate from me but had the bigger picture and was pure, silent love.

I remember having a distinct metaphor come to me. My life up until then had been a video game. Me, the child, had been playing and was the character in the video game, and this grand presence was always there, watching the video game. With that image came the feeling that this is what is real, this motherly/fatherly presence, this outstanding, ineffable, inconceivable love energy, this state of being, this state of consciousness, this open forehead and open heart. This is the true state and home, all else was illusion, all previous experience had been a video game. Not bad or wrong, but not the full truth. A dream. All had been a dream, and this was the truth of my identity. The "me" I had identified with, Mike, the personality, now felt like a speck, floating in this vast, benevolent awareness that arose within me, behind me, and all around me. I was but a child. And I cried. I sobbed, overwhelmed.

I opened. My feet opened, my palms opened, my heart opened, my forehead opened and was an eye, a light eye, and I say light eye because that is what it felt like. My body thrilled with this unspeakable love and I became a fountain for it. It flowed through me. When I finally sat up and gazed around at my surroundings, I saw that it flowed through all. This love-light in me was the love-light in everything, and now that I was open, all was open.

It is difficult for me to describe. Everything still appeared as it did before, but it all shimmered with a light that was faster or above the visible light that I was used to. Something, like a distant tree, was still distant, but also was not. It was also extremely close, nearly touching my eye, because the shimmering light that it was, was there in the distance, and was also right here, right in front of my light eye. Everything was One light, all was One thing, totally connected, but the objects and people where still there as they were before as if superimposed over the One light.

My sobbing began to slow down as I sat and gazed, awestruck. My breathing slowed. I was still on the phone with mother. Naturally, she was concerned, hearing her son cry for fifteen minutes so hard he couldn't respond. I assured her I was more than OK. I remember realizing, this is going to go away now, this perception and state of being, at least for now. It slowly faded, as I sat underneath that blooming tree in that small park in Prague.

This eye opening forever changed my life. Nothing, no other experience, has come close to its intensity. It split me open. It shattered my previous paradigm. It was like I had been in a dark closet all my life, using a candle to see, then was suddenly carried up and out and dropped onto a mountaintop in the blazing sun with a view of a gorgeous valley below me.

This experience made it undeniably clear that life is a dream, and that reality and the self are One thing. There is no separation. It made it experientially clear that everything is One. Everything was my own heart. It made all crystal clear yet simultaneously even more mysterious. It made me realize how I knew nothing about myself and reality.

I had heard of the third eye before the episode in Prague, while exploring Kundalini Yoga and chakras during my research, but I never attempted to activate it. It opened suddenly, without me willing it and without effort, like my previous heart openings. I was not meditating, nor had I intended for it to happen. It all happened on its own. Certain secret knowledge of the third eye, nor laser focus were necessary. I never paid much attention to it, or to any other chakra for that matter, nor did I believe that it was an eye, or at least acted like an eye. I took the words "third eye" as a metaphor for mental visualization. My experience obviously changed all that. Now there is no doubt. Direct experience changes everything.

The Kundalini energy seems to activate and move without me consciously telling it to and without me willing it. It is a higher power.

> "The action of the upward spiraling light drawn by the will to meet the inner light of the one infinite Creator may be likened to the beating of the heart and the movement of the muscles surrounding the lungs and all the other functions of the

> parasympathetic nervous system. The calling of the adept may be likened to those nerve and muscle actions over which the mind/body/spirit complex has conscious control."
> –*The Law of One, Book 3*

My heart openings and my third eye experience all arose after a heightened emotional state that led to a mental surrender. I surrender to a building vibration within my heart. I let it take over. It then opens my heart and light eye and fills my body. I did not open the heart or eye, the energy within me did. I aligned to its vibration by letting go, and then it did the work. The high vibration feels like my real identity, like my true home. It is within, and these experiences occur when I lighten up and allow myself to align with that high vibration. This idea of letting go and surrendering is one of the 9 truths I discovered.

Kundalini Yoga, as touched upon earlier, describes the necessity of the union of male and female energies within the body to attain enlightenment.

> "All the authorities on Kundalini Yoga are agreed about the reality of the ambrosial current, which irrigates the seventh center in the brain at the moment of the union of Shakti with Shiva, the superconscious principle behind the embodied self, and it is said that the flow of the nectar into it or into one of the lower centers on the spinal axis is always accompanied by a most exquisite rapture impossible to describe, exceeding many times in intensity that most pleasurable of bodily sensations, the orgasm, which marks the climax of sexual union."
> –Gopi Krishna, *Living with Kundalini: The autobiography of Gopi Krishna*

This description of orgasmic union of the opposite energies of the male and the female, or Shiva and Shakti, fascinate me even more now than when I originally studied them because this is exactly what it felt like when my third eye opened. It felt like an orgasm, but ten times the intensity and pleasure, and not in the genitals but in the center of my head.

The third eye is real. It is amazing how little we know about this intimate part of ourselves. We do not seek to open it and experience it because we are oblivious to its truth even while it is literally right smack in the center of our heads.

We should all be excited to experience it. It is like nothing else.

With it open, I literally saw the light. I saw the divine light in everything, and I was that same divine light. My true being and essence was love-light, and it was the true being and essence of everything all around me. I not only emotionally felt like I had entered heaven, paradise, our true home like I had in previous heart openings, but now I saw it. I experienced it inside of me and outside of me.

It is all still very mysterious to me, but I cannot deny my experience.

Since that initial awakening and opening of my third eye, it has opened again several times. There have been times when it suddenly blinks when I blink my two eyes, without any apparent cause, and I am startled by the sensation.

There are times when I have felt it open and blink several times when I was incredibly angry. This fascinates me, because I never thought such an emotion would activate it, since the initial awakening of it was so blissful. When this happened, the anger I felt was because I witnessed an injustice done to another. I became angry, and it blinked. It seems any strong emotion of the heart that is pure and not of a lower nature opens it. But honestly, I do not know, at least not yet. Like I said, it is still very mysterious to me.

Then there are times when it opens when I do breathwork or pranayama, meaning in Sanskrit "breath control," or control of prana. Prana is considered the vital energy that is in everything, the cosmic force, the fuel of all life. Pranayama is a crucial part and practice of Yoga. It is a discipline of various breathing techniques. My third eye has activated almost every time I have done deep, rhythmic, rapid breathing over a period of at least 10 minutes and have allowed myself to feel strong emotions of love and peace. This is the only action I have discovered thus far that I can willfully do and have it open.

> "Focusing vital breath between the brows, one attains the supreme divine spirit of man."
> –Krishna, *Bhagavad-Gita*, trans. Barbara Stoler Miller[4]

To be clear, I, the personality self, the small self, the ego, does not open the light eye. The energy within me does, and deep breathing seems to increase the flow of energy within me. I highly recommend breathwork and/or pranayama. Nothing gets me to that high state of being as quickly as breathing rhythmically and deeply.

There was another eye opening I had that is worth mentioning.

I was participating in a deep breathwork class at the Lightening in a Bottle music festival held in California. It had been a long time since I had felt the third eye. I had strayed from the spiritual path ever since a challenging experience I had (The Nightmare). I still read and researched occasionally, but not as passionately as before.

A group of about thirty festival goers and I all lay in the grass below a large, twisting oak tree. The leader of the group guided us through the session, instructing us on how to take deep, belly-filling breaths and quick, full exhales. Music played and we all began.

Halfway into it, a song came on with moving lyrics, and I felt the familiar heart pressure. I quietly began to weep. All these instances when I begin to cry are from awe-inspiring levels of love felt in the heart and body. I then sobbed. The sobbing was a similar breath pattern to the deep breathing that was instructed. The breathwork matched the rhythm and depth of the sobbing I had experienced before in Prague and the other previous heart openings, so it seemed to initiate the state again. This incident made me realize that the sobbing during all my heart openings was basically the same breathing as certain pranayama exercises and most deep breathwork. I sobbed and again felt the heart release. The heart's energy coursed through my body and to up my head. The eye opened.

---

[4] Excerpt(s) from THE BHAGAVAD-GITA: KRISHNA'S COUNSEL IN TIME OF WAR by Barbara Miller, translation copyright © 1986 by Barbara Stoler Miller. Used by permission of Bantam Books, an imprint of Random House, a division of Penguin Random House LLC. All rights reserved.

In this state, I am in silent amazement. The word grace comes to mind: a silent state of innocent grace. Everything shined with vibrating love-light.

The session ended with the entire group huddling and holding hands. I continued to weep, and I looked around me and at others in wonder. A beautiful young woman was sitting beside me, holding my hand. I looked at her and she looked at me. She smiled and kissed my forehead, kissed the exact location of my third eye that was trembling and glistening. I felt a profound love for humanity, for earth. Everyone around me felt like my family. All was love. All *is* love.

The third eye is popular in the New Age spiritual movement. The rise of Yoga in the west has helped to bring more awareness to it. A search on YouTube or Google will result in a plethora of content. You will find instructions on how to open it, advice to stop consuming things that contain fluoride, and lists of crystals that help activate it. This is all very amusing to me because I am reminded of how we really have no idea. Its power melted me into a sobbing baby. All previous thoughts of what I was and what reality was were obliterated by its grace. All we can do is surrender our heart to this unimaginable energy within us. Everything else seems like we are fussing with twigs and matches. All the while the truth is a giant bonfire, already lit and burning an inconceivably brilliant and infinite light.

The terms "chakra" and the "third eye" are way overused and misused, to the point of becoming a cliché. I cringe when I hear it over and over again in flippant ways… We have forgotten what we truly are.

After the opening of my third eye, I have no doubt of the truth of Yoga's chakras, and their role in the attainment of enlightenment, yet there is a lot of misleading information out there about them. Look within. Trust and rely on your own experience of the intelligence within your heart.

I also like to call the third eye the forehead eye or the light eye, because the term "third eye" for most is just a metaphor and does not represent an actual part of us that acts like an eye. It is like our familiar eyes, because it provides sight, but instead of providing sight of the light in our known, visible spectrum, it provides sight of the usually invisible love-light in all things, the once hidden unity of all.

In Yoga, the light eye is the 6th chakra, called ajna. As the Kundalini rises, this is the last energy center it passes through before reaching sahasrara, the crown of the head, the end goal and location of apotheosis.

> "The solar and lunar nadis intersect with sushumna at the various chakras. Finally at the ajna chakra, the place between the eyebrows, Kundalini takes command of the mental functions, opening a new channel of perception, the sixth sense or Third Eye, signifying the ascent to a higher step of the evolutionary ladder on the part of the successful initiate. From the ajna chakra, ida and pingala, as is said, proceed to the right and left nostrils respectively, and the sushumna enters the sahasrara."
> –Gopi Krishna, *Kundalini: The Secret of Yoga*

> "Ajna, the lotus of 'Command," located between the eyebrows, is what we could call the chakra of heaven, the highest in the world of incarnate forms. The forms of the pharaohs from Egypt show the Uraeus Serpent coming out of this point between the brows. When the Kundalini has reached this point, one beholds God."
> –Joseph Campbell, *Reflections on the Art of Living*[5]

> "When the Kundalini reaches Chakra VI, you see God: 'Brahman with characteristics.' At Chakra VII, you go past God and are in the transcendent: 'Brahman without characteristics.'"
> –Joseph Campbell, *Reflections on the Art of Living*

> "The God that has been dormant in muladhara is here [in ajna] fully awake, the only reality; and therefore this center had been called the condition in which one unites with Shiva. One could say it was the center of the *unio mystica* with the power of God…"
> –Carl G. Jung, *The Psychology of Kundalini Yoga*

---

[5] From Joseph Campbell's *Reflections on the Art of Living, A Joseph Campbell Companion* Copyright © Joseph Campbell Foundation (jcf.org) 1991. Used with permission.

The light eye or ajna chakra opens the individual to a new perception that allows them to see God, or Brahman, within and as the identity of all the diversity of manifestation.

Each chakra location has been attributed to a corresponding endocrine gland or organ. The third eye's is the pineal gland, which is part of the epithalamus in the brain. It is located at the center of the head, between the brain's hemispheres. Its location corresponds to my experience.

Rene Descartes called the pineal gland the seat of the soul. It produces serotonin, melatonin, and is hypothesized to produce DMT, or dimethyltryptamine. DMT has been referred to as the "spirit molecule." It is found in nearly every plant and animal. It can be taken as a psychedelic and has been for centuries by shamans in South America in the form of ayahuasca. DMT is produced and released in humans during sleep, creating dream states. It is also released during birth, death, near-death experiences, and spiritual awakenings.

In some reptiles and amphibians, the pineal gland is linked to a parietal eye that is photoreceptive and located at top of their heads. When I look at pictures of reptiles' and toads' parietal eyes, I feel a funny sensation in my forehead, like a slight vibration, as if when I behold the light eye in something else, it starts to activate again. It mysteriously recognizes itself and responses.

Symbols representing the third eye and the Kundalini energy that activate it can be found in ancient artwork all over the globe. There is the Eye of Horus, and the snake head between the eyes of King Tutankhamun's pharaoh mask in Egyptian culture. There is the bindi in Hindu culture. Buddha is almost always depicted in artwork and sculptures with a mark on the center of his forehead. Even in today's culture third eye symbology can be found. The United States' one-dollar bill has a pyramid with an all-seeing eye on the top. Does this perhaps represent the truth of our divine nature?

The process of the rising energy through the body's energy centers to the forehead eye is not only found in Yoga. As the next two quotes reveal, the Chinese San Bao, or three treasures, and the Indian Granthis, or three knots, are different names for the exact same steps in the inner journey. The Taoists share the same method as the Yogis for enlightenment.

"In China the three qualities of man's energy are called the San Bao, or 'three treasures.' They are ching, ch'i, and shen, or essence, energy, and consciousness. By transmutation of the three treasures from coarse to subtle form, and by subsequent interaction, a mysterious 'something' is conceived. That 'something' is the spirit embryo, which, like any baby, requires further gestation prior to final birth. However, should the Taoist yogi be successful in developing the spirit body, he can exist independent of his physical body and is as such immortal. … Once ching had been transmuted to ch'i through meditation and yogic breathing, the practitioner discarded the entanglements of mundane life and 'sought stillness' so that he could further enliven the shen through the ch'i. (Reportedly, the area where the seedling shen resides is between and behind the eyebrows – the third eye to some.) But once the shen was conceived it had to gestate; once gestated it had to be born; once born it required nourishment. … For the Taoist alchemist, the dantien [three finger widths below navel] was the crucible in which the elixir of immortality was brewed. It was there that ching was refined into ch'i, while from the dantien purified ch'i was sent up to the 'Spirit Valley' between the eyebrows to give birth to the embryo shen. … There was a step further from that point on if the yogi truly desired eternity: The independent shen had to be merged with the Source of All Things, the Tao. In essence, what the teachers were saying was that the personality had to unite with the flow of the whole universe."
–Kosta Danaos, *The Magus of Java*

"There are three main knots in the sushumna [the path up the center of the body] that represent the three aspects of consciousness: knowing, feeling, and doing. The Brahma Granthi is feeling and the mind; the Vishnu Granthi is doing and prana; and Rudra Granthi is knowing and jnana (true knowledge). When the three knots are untied, phenomenal reality becomes pervaded by divine energy and the self becomes established in the Sheath of Bliss. Brahma Granthi … most

tantric scriptures place it in the Manipura Chakra, the third chakra … Vishnu Granthi is located in the area of Anahata Center (heart center), which is also the seat of prana … Rudra Granthi is located in the area of the Ajna Chakra, the area of the third eye. Rudra is the destroyer and is true knowledge. There is nothing to destroy except the illusion that is I-consciousness or ego … Finally, one must get beyond the attachment to I-consciousness, which obstructs the path of Kundalini on its way to Soma Chakra where the supreme truth is realized and non-dual consciousness is achieved. The I-consciousness is like 'drop-consciousness' and the truth is the ocean of pure consciousness. The drop and the ocean are one, but the I-consciousness of the drop keeps it separated."
–Harish Johari, *Chakras*[6]

I enjoy finding the similarities of spiritual ideas between cultures, especially between east and west. I believe that my experience in Prague gave me a glimpse into what Jesus referred to as the kingdom of heaven.

Of course, I do not know if Jesus even existed. But if he did, it is my belief that Christianity, whether intentionally or innocently, has incorrectly interpreted him.

I believe he was a man, a loving, forgiving, peaceful, enlightened man, that realized who and what he truly was and then expressed that truth in his life. Yes, he was the son of God, but so is everyone and everything. I believe he was the way-shower, and the prime example of what humans are capable of. He was showing the rest of humanity what they too could be and what they too could do.

"Is it not written in your law, 'I said, ye are gods,'?"
–Jesus, John 10:34, *The Holy Bible King James Version*

---

[6] *Chakras* by Harish Johari published by Inner Traditions International and Bear & Company, ©2000. All rights reserved. http://www.Innertraditions.com Reprinted with permission of publisher.

> "Verily, verily, I say unto you, he that believeth on me, the works that I do shall he do also; and greater works than these shall he do."
> –Jesus, John 14:12, *The Holy Bible King James Version*

The kingdom of heaven that he often referred to, I believe, is the state of consciousness of the awareness and perception of the One, of the love-light, or of Creator, in everything. It is not something that comes later after death. It is here and now within us and all around us. I believe this kingdom is what I momentarily experienced when my light eye opened.

The Gospel of Thomas is non-canonical and was found in Nag Hammadi, Egypt in 1945 among many other ancient Christian texts that now form what is called the Nag Hammadi Library. Scholars believe it sheds light onto Jesus' sayings. It is my favorite text regarding Jesus. If you read it compared to the Bible as we now know it, it feels much different. What Jesus says in the Gospel of Thomas seems much more aligned with the rest of the overall themes of other spiritual texts.

> "'When will the kingdom come?' 'It will not be said, Look here it is, or, Look there it is. Rather, the father's kingdom is spread out upon the earth, and people do not see it.'"
> –Jesus, Gospel of Thomas, *The Nag Hammadi Library*

When I first read this quote, it blew my mind. What is he saying? The kingdom is here and now, and it is inside of you and all around you. People do not see it because they have forgotten what they are. Know yourself and you will realize that you are not separate from the energy, the love-light that is everything, but are connected like father and son.

> "If those who lead you say to you, 'See, the kingdom is in the sky,' then the birds of the sky will precede you. If they say to you, 'It is in the sea,' then the fish will precede you. Rather, the kingdom is inside of you, and it is outside of you. When you come to know yourselves, then you will become known, and you will realize that it is you who are the sons of the living father."
> –Jesus, Gospel of Thomas, *The Nag Hammadi Library*

The "living father" is *living*; it is present and active. It is here and now, and we are not separate from it. I believe we experience this union, visually see, and know the "living father," through the light eye.

> "The light of the body is the eye: If therefore thine eye be single, thy whole body shall be full of light."
> –Jesus, Matthew 6:22, *The Holy Bible King James Version*

Most would probably take this quote as a metaphor, especially since Jesus seemed to be fond of them, and of allegories and parables. But after my experience, I cannot ignore how it directly acknowledges the third eye and the sensation of light in the body.

> "Whoever has ears, let him hear. There is light within man of light, and he lights up the whole world. If he (or: it) does not shine, he is darkness."
> –Jesus, Gospel of Thomas, *The Nag Hammadi Library*

When you make your eye single, your body fills with light. When your body fills with light, it lights up the entire world. This is exactly what my experience felt like. The energy filled my body, opened my single eye, and then I saw the same energy in all my surroundings. The light in me turned on and lit up everything around me.

> "When you make the two one, and when you make the inside like the outside, and the above like the below, and when you make the male and the female one in the same, so that the male not be male nor the female female; and when you fashion eyes in place of an eye, and a hand in place of a hand, and a foot in place of a foot, and a likeness in place of a likeness; then you will enter the Kingdom."
> –Jesus, Gospel of Thomas, *The Nag Hammadi Library*

Entering the kingdom is entering the state of consciousness where everything, absolutely everything, all of manifestation, every opposite included, every being and thing regardless of how it presents itself, is recognized and treated as the Creator. Everything is One: One energy, One consciousness, One love. The kingdom is not a distinct location but is all around us and within us. It is every location. It is the love-light vibration that permeates, and that is the foundation of, everything. You enter it by raising your perception and vibration to see, feel, and fully experience that love-light in all. In a sense, all you do is remember what you and everything else have always been all along. This idea is the true essence and foundation of all religions and of spirituality in general.

> "Realize that heaven is a perfect state of consciousness, a perfect world here and now, and all we need to do is accept it. It is here all about us, waiting for us to open the inner eye. Through that eye our bodies shall be made light, the light which is neither of the sun or the moon but of the Father; and the Father is right here in the very inner most part of our being."
> –Baird T. Spalding, *Life and Teaching of the Masters of the Far East V.1*

> "The awakened pineal gland is like an eye that opens into higher-dimensional reality. It is our point of contact with the new Christ consciousness grid that is energizing the planet and leading it towards its rebirth on the fourth dimension."
> –Bob Frissell, *You are a Spiritual Being Having a Human Experience*[7]

> "See all the universe, animate and inanimate, and whatever else you wish to see, all stands as one in my body. But you cannot see me with your own eye. I will give you a divine eye to see the majesty of my discipline."
> –Krishna, *Bhagavad-Gita*, trans. Barbara Stoler Miller

> "The 'kingdom of heaven' is not something lying 'above the earth' or coming 'after death.' It does not have a yesterday or a

---

[7] From *You Are a Spiritual Being Having a Human Experience* by Bob Frissell published by Frog Books/North Atlantic Books, copyright © 2001 by Bob Frissell. Reprinted by permission of North Atlantic Books.

day after tomorrow, and it will not arrive in a 'thousand years.' It is an experience of the heart. It is everywhere and it is nowhere."
–Friedrich Nietzsche, *The Anti-christ*

"The Kingdom is the awareness of the creator in all things."
–Paul Selig, *The Book of Mastery*[8]

"The God you thought of as distant will take up residence in your heart. The heaven that you were taught is far away will rest at your fingertips."
–*Emmanuel's Book III: What is an Angel doing here?* [9]

"In Him I have acquired eyes and have seen His holy day."
–Odes of Solomon, Ode 15, *The Lost Books of the Bible and the forgotten books of Eden*

"The eye with which I see God is the same with which God sees me. My eye and God's eye is one eye, and one sight, and one knowledge, and one love."
–Meister Eckhart

"It is true that this light is from heaven, as heaven is all about us and is light vibration. The actual focal center or starting point of heaven must be right within my body. Therefore, this heavenly light must come forth from me. The I AM of me must allow this light essence to come in … It is the God-power, which is recognized all about you, allowed to come in, be generated and transformed within your body, then sent out through the

---

[8] Excerpt(s) from THE BOOK OF MASTERY: THE MASTERY TRILOGY: BOOK I by Paul Selig, copyright © 2016 by Paul Selig. Used by permission of TarcherPerigee, an imprint of the Penguin Publishing Group, a division of Penguin Random House LLC . All rights reserved.

[9] Excerpt(s) from EMMANUEL'S BOOK III: WHAT IS AN ANGEL DOING HERE? compiled by by Pat Rodegast and Judith Stanton, copyright © 1994 by Pat Rodegast and Judith Stanton. Used by permission of Bantam Books, an imprint of Random House, a division of Penguin Random House LLC. All rights reserved.

> reflector. These things are readily accomplished by all when they stand forth as God, their divine heritage, the Christ of God, all One. This is the divine and definite motto for all humanity. The closer humanity draws to this great healing ray, the earlier will discord and inharmony be erased. If you live freely in this light vibration which is the light of the whole world, and all draw near to it, the closer you will draw to man's true abiding-place. Thus you find that I AM is the light of the whole world. Behold God, the table is spread. Lift up this mighty one God, this I AM. Lift this body to God and you and all are crowned Lord of All. You do place the crown upon your own head. None can do this for you."
>
> –Baird T. Spalding, *Life and Teaching of the Masters of the Far East V.3*

With my third eye open, I saw everything as light. Not only did I see it, I felt it in my heart. While in that state, there is no question that all is One. My heart was ablaze with this love-light, this light of the world, and its power was so humbling, so true, and good, I could do or think nothing, just weep.

> "My heart was cloven and there appeared a flower, and grace sprang up, and fruit from the Lord, for the highest one split me with his holy spirit, exposed my love for him and filled me with his love. His splitting of my heart was my salvation and I followed the way of his peace, the way of truth."
>
> –Odes of Solomon, *The Nag Hammadi Library*

I adore this passage. It poetically describes the feeling of the heart cracking open and filling the body with love. This is exactly what it feels like. Feeling and seeing this is like being reborn.

> "Every midwife knows that not until a mother's womb softens from the pain of labor will a way unfold and the infant find that opening to be born. Oh friend! There is a treasure in your heart, it is heavy with child. Listen. All the awakened ones, like trusted

midwives, are saying, welcome this pain, it opens the dark passage of Grace."
–Rumi, *One Song,* trans. Coleman Barks

Another passage that sends goosebumps up and down my body when I read it. It is very relatable. It perfectly describes the sensation of my heart openings. They all start with slight pain in the heart, and when I surrender and loosen, the pain releases and in a state of indescribable grace I become what feels like a child of light. I feel reborn because as the third eye opens, all is made new. A new world of love and light is revealed.

"The True Self in her realization makes all things new."
–Paul Selig, *The Book of Freedom*[10]

Of all the spiritual beliefs and practices that I have read, Yoga is the most aligned to my experiences. Therefore, I focused my research on Yoga. It provides a road map to the inner world and its energies. It is a system for humanity to evolve in consciousness and reach enlightenment. I recommend the exploration of Yoga whole heartedly.

However, I believe there are many paths that lead to the awakening of the light eye, to the opening of the heart, and to enlightenment.

I have shared my path. That does not mean it is the only path. Even though I was led to Yoga by my visions, I did not actively practice the exercises that Kundalini Yoga prescribes. I researched them passionately but did not do them regularly. I just kept researching. The unfoldment of my beautiful experience was not initiated by meditation, pranayama, or asanas, but by a surrender to a rise of emotion. Ultimately my allowance of an alignment to the heart and its strong emotion of overpowering, unconditional love is what did it. I did not become that special something, the special something became me.

That is how it happened for me, but I believe there are many possible ways for it to open. I believe there is not one ideology and method that is the only way. We are all the same energy, yet, paradoxically, we are all unique.

---

[10] Excerpt(s) from THE BOOK OF FREEDOM by Paul Selig, copyright © 2018 by Paul Selig. Used by permission of Tarcher, an imprint of Penguin Publishing Group, a division of Penguin Random House LLC. All rights reserved.

That is what makes earth so beautiful. You should be wary of any belief system that claims it and only it is the correct path. Find your own way. Listen to your heart.

The Nightmare

> "Never regret thy fall,
> O Icarus of the fearless flight
> For the greatest tragedy of them all
> Is never to feel the burning light."
> –Oscar Wilde

The Mirror

As I present the one identity
as I express and feel and vision-think
and be the me that I am meant to be
and be true light of self, in one eye's blink
reality is shaped and formed based on
my own established state of heart and mind
and therefore, all is paradise: heaven
ubiquitous and now. But when unkind
and troubled storm of thoughts diversified
become a crashing riot in the brain
my own subjective is objectified
and my surrounding dream a hellish game.
All outer trouble mirrors inner lack.
What you put forth is what you receive back.

I've said it before, and I'll say it again: the opening of my third eye changed my life. However, at first, I continued doing everything the same as before. I kept the experience to myself, except for my mother and sister. I went on with life. I attended school the following fall semester at Naropa, but I began to grow restless. I began questioning everything, "Should I even go to school anymore? All I should focus on is fully establishing that state of consciousness and open perception within me, right? I should place all my focus on the third eye, right?" I felt alone in my experience. I feared ridicule, disbelieve, and apathy from my classmates and friends. I dropped out after that semester. I attended University of Utah briefly and figured I could continue my research but still attend school but at a more affordable cost. It did not feel right. How could I sit in lecture halls after my experience? I dropped out from there too shortly after.

I started freaking out, but quietly and internally. Looking back, I cannot help but sigh and shake my head. Why was I freaking out? At times I wished I had never left Naropa University, but all has its purpose. I guess I needed the experience that was coming.

I was growing anxious and wanted another spiritual break through. It had been a year and a half since my third eye experience. I was pushing myself. I was becoming frantic. Again, looking back, I do not exactly know why. I wish I would have just relaxed.

I set an intention to do a fast in a darkened room. I stayed in the room for 24 hours, but after coming out the fast and the stillness persisted and seemed to take over me. I had a growing feeling of impending doom. I stopped speaking and eating. I would sit and stare. I did not sleep for three, maybe four days.

I feel badly for what I put my mom and stepdad through during that time. I was unresponsive. My state of mind got dark. I went into fear. It was all very trippy. My thoughts started to become frightening. I could not snap out of it. Reality was becoming dreamlike, and I was sinking into fear, thus it became a waking nightmare. Things began to happen that I cannot explain. I could faintly hear people's thoughts and feel their fears. I would have a thought, and something would happen that directly corresponded to the thought in my reality. I was stuck in a fantasy of my own creation.

I will not go into all the details of what I was experiencing and thinking, but I will give one example of my thoughts manifesting. I flew from my mom and stepdad's place to stay with another relative. While on the plane, I started thinking of a person pregnant with a demon. I know, insane. I was in a crazy head space. As I thought this, my belly began to swell. It grew to resemble a pregnant belly. I remember watching my seatbelt become tight around my waist. I rushed to the airplane bathroom and sat on the toilet and released what felt like diarrhea. When I finished and looked down into the bowl, I saw it was filled with blood... My thoughts were instantaneously affecting my body and creating my reality experience. Things like this kept happening.

In Yoga, specifically in Patanjali's Yoga sutras, there are 9 obstacles on the spiritual path. One of them is called Bhranti Darshana. It is hallucination or getting stuck in an imaginative narrative of the mind. I hit this obstacle in a head-on collision.

No one knew what to do with me. I was eventually hospitalized for a week and diagnosed with schizophrenia, bi-polar disease, and mania. I was treated as a psychotic and given many medications. Western medicine does not consider such things as spiritual awakenings and psychic trauma. What I needed was a master or guide to help me through it, but instead was heavily sedated.

I experienced what has been called Kundalini syndrome, Kundalini psychosis, or a spiritual emergency. This can occur when an individual is not yet ready for such an expansion of perception and power, yet they rush into it, over eager to progress. I obviously had awakened a power within me during my third eye opening, yet I was not ready or mature enough for such a power. Fear took over, put me onto a tailspin, and sent my psyche reeling.

> "There exist spontaneous non-ordinary states that would in the west be seen and treated as psychosis, treated mostly by suppressive medication. But if we use the observations from the study of non-ordinary states, and also from other spiritual traditions, they should really be treated as crises of transformation, or crises of spiritual opening. Something that should really be supported rather than suppressed. If properly understood and properly supported, they are actually conducive to healing and transformation."
>
> –Stanislav Grof, MD. "The Frontiers of the Mind" *healthy.net*

> "Episodes of this kind [spiritual emergencies] have been described in sacred literature of all ages as a result of meditative practices and as signposts of the mystical path."
> –Stanislov and Christina Grof, *Spiritual Emergency: When Personal Transformation Becomes a Crisis*

The well-known, at least in yogic circles, Gopi Krishna, in his book *Living with Kundalini, Autobiography of Gopi Krishna,* describes his famous experience of his Kundalini awakening. At times, the phenomena he endured were very unbalanced, unpleasant, and even horrific.

> "The days that followed [his Kundalini awakening] had all the appearance of a prolonged nightmare. It seemed as if I had abruptly precipitated myself from the steady rock of normality into a madly racing whirlpool of abnormal existence. … The nights were even more terrible. I could not bear to have a light in my room after I had retired to bed. The moment my head touched the pillow a large tongue of flame spread across my spine into the interior of my head. It appeared as if the stream of living light continuously rushing through the spinal cord into the cranium gathered greater speed and volume during the hours of darkness. … Sometimes it seemed as if a jet of molten copper, mounting up through the spine, dashed against my crown and fell in a scintillating shower of vast dimensions all around me. I gazed at it fascinated, with fear gripping my heart."
> –Gopi Krishna, *Living with Kundalini, The Autobiography of Gopi Krishna*

This spiritual emergency affected me for years following it. In my naïveté, I believed that I had failed spirit and that I had fallen from grace. My one-pointed goal and passion was now seen by me as a failure. I became depressed. I went back to school. I started smoking, drinking, numbing out. I was lost. I wish I could go back and slap myself and yell, "Snap out of it! You're fine! Get excited again! Don't you remember what you've seen, what you've felt! You know what is possible. Wake up!"

Why did this happen? I was forcing myself. I was becoming impatient, anxious, and indecisive. I was too much in my head. I proceeded hurriedly, without being humble, without love, gratitude, and peace. The psychic awakening happened, but not the way I would have preferred. It happened with fear.

The positive side of this ordeal was that I experienced without a doubt that our thoughts create our bodies, surroundings, and reality, more so than I had ever thought possible. Our thoughts and perceptions essentially *are* our reality. I realized this truth and experienced the power of thought firsthand but in a frightening way. Our reality is a wonderful dream or a nightmare, all depending on our thoughts and beliefs.

What is going on inside of you, inside your mind and heart, creates circumstances outside of you, because what is outside of you really isn't outside of you. It is an extension of what you are. Thus, as you are, so all shall be around you. Your perception makes everything as it seems to be. This is yet another one of the 9 truths: You create your reality.

The warning I received in my second snake vision was regarding this mental trauma I eventually had. "Be careful, that is where the head is." What this means is once this power and energy rises to the head, your power of manifesting, creating, and attracting what you think of will accelerate. Things thought up will appear and happen instantaneously in reality. With this power comes great responsibility. Therefore, beware, or be aware of what you think of. Be in love, not in fear. The will of the ego should be quieted so that the will of love, the will of the One in all things, may be heard and done. If the will of the personality, with its personal fears and desires, still holds sway it will invite great imbalance.

Jesus and the Buddha were both tempted to use their newly acclaimed power and perception from a place of desire and fear, to operate from their lower nature and individualistic thinking. This was necessary before they reached their full, true self-realization. Jesus was tempted in the desert by the devil. Buddha was tempted by Mara while he sat under the Bodhi tree. Both went through three trials. The temptations represent the change necessary from personal will to the will of the whole, the change of operating from the mortal self to the eternal being at the root of all selves, the change of perspective from the seemingly separate body's viewpoint to the big picture of Creator seeing all as Creator. Only while still in the limited mindset and perspective of the ego can a person fear and desire.

Perhaps this was a test, a threshold to see if I was truly ready to be fully established in an awakened state. Turns out, I was not.

Siddhis, a Yogic term, are spiritual and supernatural powers that awaken when one reaches higher states of consciousness on the path to enlightenment. If prematurely awakened, these can be too much to bear. One such Siddhi is being able to hear other people's thoughts. Imagine having this ability. It certainly would drive most insane, if not prepared for it. I believe I awakened some Siddhis that I was most definitely not ready for.

My vision was a warning to not rush but to allow the process of the evolution of consciousness to happen naturally and in a balanced way, with love as the foundation of every step.

If you are on the spiritual path, do not push forward too quickly as I did. Let the unfolding happen naturally. Always have love as the foundation and main motivating force for your journey.

I was trying to reach up and grab that higher state of being that I had experienced in Prague. This is not the way. One does not force themselves into alignment but allows themselves to be aligned. One surrenders.

Ubiquitous Rites of Passage

It took several years to shake the psychic trauma I had. I eventually snapped out of it and continued my spiritual search, but only more recently.

Why did I get so frantic and desperate? What could have prevented my spiritual breakdown?

A few years after my waking nightmare, I stumbled upon rites of passage among indigenous tribes while doing research for college. (I eventually went back to school and finished.) I love finding the shared themes of different belief systems and cultures, so I continued to research and found that the majority of earth's indigenous cultures, ranging from locations such as the African plains, to the Amazon jungle, to the Australian outback, held ceremonies signifying and initiating the change from childhood to adulthood within a developing human being. This, I believe, is what I needed, and perhaps could have prevented the whole ordeal.

These rites of passage, initiations, coming of age rituals, vision quests, and puberty rites, provided the once mother-needy young adult with a grander sense of his or her own purpose and responsibility to the community and to his or her own Source. They provided answers to the crucial questions a young adult has, just as I did, while growing up in this world: who am I, why am I here, what is the true nature of this reality, what is my purpose, what is my role, how do I operate in this world, and what is expected of me? The similarities of the structure and intention between the rites of passage of the drastically different cultures are profound.

Today, specifically in the United States, because that is the culture I know the best, there is a lack of such ceremonies, causing youth to seek out their own, at times, more harmful rites of passage without a support group to assist and mentor.

The multitudinous, yet harmonious in purpose and structure, rites of passage from indigenous cultures worldwide reveal the psychological and spiritual need for developing young adults, especially now in this modern age, to experience outwardly, symbolically, what is occurring within them: a transformation from small, ego self to big, cosmic Self.

> "At a certain point in life, society asks this dependent little creature to become a responsible initiator of action [...] The function of puberty rites in cultures older than our own was to effect a psychological transformation"
> –Joseph Campbell, *Pathways to Bliss*

Joseph Campbell was a master on the subject at hand. He compared the myths of all the world's cultures and pointed out the fundamental foundations that they all shared. Humans, he says, are born too soon. They are like kangaroos; they depend heavily on their parents until they develop fully, quite some time after birth. Leaving the second womb, or the pouch in the case of the mother kangaroo, is like a rebirth.

Campbell's monomyth in his well-known work, *The Hero with a Thousand Faces*, borrows the same pattern found in puberty rites:

> "The mythological adventure of the hero is a magnification of the formula represented in the rites of passage: separation-initiation- return."
> –Joseph Campbell, *The Hero with a Thousand Faces*[11]

This same structure was summarized by Arnold van Gennup, who set the standard for cultural anthropologists in describing the steps in tribal rites: separation, transition, and incorporation. Essentially, the child separates from his accustomed comforts, such as his mother and home, is initiated by elders in some usually traumatic and dramatic way, such as circumcision, and then returns to his normal life, transformed. This structure, in the context of rites of passage, is ubiquitous. The separation is necessary so that the young

---

[11] From Joseph Campbell's *The Hero with a Thousand Faces* Copyright © Joseph Campbell Foundation (jcf.org) 2008. Used with permission.

adult stands alone without the familiar and dependable. Then, the initiation itself is often scary and jarring.

> "The meaning ... behind these rituals of confusion and strangeness is the understanding that there is a tendency in all of us to prefer the familiar, out of habit and security. ... The disorientation does not allow for turning back to the previous state"
> –Edith Sullwold, "Swimming With Seals: The Developmental Role Of Initiation Rituals In Work With Adolescents." *Child & Youth Care Forum*

The most interesting example I came across in my research is an initiation done by the Aranda in Central Australia. When an Aranda boy is between ten and twelve, he is taken by the men in the tribe and tossed into the air several times while the women scream and cry around them. The elder men then paint on his chest and tell him that he is now the "living counterpart" of his "mythological ancestor" (Campbell *Masks of God* 88). The boy from then on does not gather food with the women, but hunts with the men. More importantly, the boy's source and place of birth is transferred from his mother to the sky. He is reborn: "the concept of the ego has expanded … beyond the biography of his physical body" (89). From then on, the boy recognizes his reality as a dream, or as the altjeringa, the dreamtime. "The boy is himself a mythological, eternal being who has become incarnate" (89). The intensity of the initiation and rebirth is worth the revelation given by the elders. The boy becomes a spiritual being, and recognizes all as spiritual, or as a dream (89).

Growing young adults seek out revelations today, but modern culture does not supply them with any ritual or process. Therefore, they create their own, sometimes successfully, other times not so much. I believe the appeal of hallucinogenic substances for young adults is a healthy desire to transform their ego, to open their minds, and to feel their connection with the universe. Plant medicine has been used in indigenous cultures for centuries for communing with the spirit world and for initiations. Without a provided ceremony from their "tribe," kids take these medicines unguided and in unsupportive environments, which can lead to further confusion, paranoia, or psychotic breaks.

Some teens haze others or themselves, perform harmful acts as initiations, or commit suicide, all in search of their rebirth into a grander sense of self.

> "Adolescent suicides could be a reflection of the element of initiation that is viewed as death of the old in order to become the new, but here the death becomes literal, not symbolic"
> –Edith Sullwold, "Swimming With Seals: The Developmental Role Of Initiation Rituals In Work With Adolescents." *Child & Youth Care Forum*

There is a need for a symbolic transformation to help a young adult establish within themselves the sexual, moral, and mental changes that take place in becoming an adult.

I feel that after my third eye experience, something like a rite of passage could have helped. I think I was subconsciously craving one. I wanted an initiation to anchor this transformation of consciousness into my body and my personality. A space was needed where I was supported, yet pushed, by family, friends, and society, to express and share the expansion of my perception, and thereby move me into a new role. Instead, no outward support or rite of passage was available, nor was I conscious that this is what I needed, so the imbalance worsened as I sank into an internal fantasy resembling a nightmare. The experience was intense and strange, like the puberty rites of indigenous tribes, thereby making it unforgettable and unignorable. I received profound revelations, no doubt, but it all could have been handled in a much more supportive way.

Today, if one has visions, grand epiphanies, and experiences direct creation through witnessing their own thoughts manifest instantly within the circumstances around them, they are, just as I was, shoved into psych-wards, diagnosed with mania and schizophrenia, and medicated until dumb and numb. In an indigenous culture, such experiences would be seen by elders as a young adult being reborn into his true role of being a shaman, medicine man, or simply a spiritual being who recognizes his or her own creator-abilities and source. In Joseph Campbell's *Myths to Live By,* in the chapter titled "Schizophrenia –the Inward Journey," he explains the similarities between what we label as schizophrenia with vision quests done by shamans:

> "The inward journeys of the mythological hero, the shaman, the mystic, and the schizophrenic are in principle the same; and when the return or remission occurs, it is experienced as a rebirth"
> –Joseph Campbell, *Myths to Live By*

The fact that so many primitive cultures had puberty rites and that they all share the same structure, reveal their necessity. Patterns universally apparent such as the separation, initiation, and integration pattern of rites of passage ceremonies, reflect patterns within the True Self, the Self of the cosmos.

For the spiritual growth of adolescents, modern society could adapt and apply certain rites of passage and initiations. Primitive cultures have already established the three-step process for us. Without them, I am afraid many other growing, young adults may be doomed to experience what I did: the opening of the spiritual world within colliding with modern medicine's cold, mechanical diagnoses.

The Pursuit of Enlightenment

"But seek first his kingdom and his righteousness, and all these things shall be yours as well."
–Jesus, Matthew 6:33, *The New Oxford Annotated Bible*

Enlightenment is possible. I know this from my heart and eye openings. To be fully established in that state of being, to be fully aware of Union, is my only goal now because nothing else compares to it. Nothing else compares to being fully open and conscious of our potential, our power, and our Source. Feeling and seeing this Love-Light in everyone, in everything, and within, is bliss.

What do we want? What do we all want in life? My answer is bliss. Some other words come to mind: joy, freedom, abundance, purpose, excitement, love, peace, connection, creativity, growth. It is my opinion that these are all characteristics of what we really are. They are all describing the One consciousness, and thus are all inherent within us. To experience them, to feel them, to find them, we must remember what we are.

If you seek these things, you should seek to know yourself. This is the pursuit of enlightenment.

We tend to put the cart before the horse and say, "I will be happy if... I will be happy when…" and fill in the blank with things or conditions that represent happiness for us, and thereby delay happiness, whereas happiness is our *true* state of being. It is what we really are. We are bliss-consciousness, love-energy, joy-light. It is not somewhere else or later. It is here and now. It is within.

The pursuit of experiencing this identity is the pursuit of enlightenment. Therefore, I say, the pursuit of enlightenment is the pursuit of happiness.

We are in control of our own state of being. The surrounding circumstances are not. A lot of people like to play victim, but that is their choice. We are impacted not by situations but by our thoughts of them. We choose how to perceive them and therefore choose how we will be affected by them. We are not victims of circumstance. We create all our experiences.

Humans want more and more and more because subconsciously they know that they are one with everything! Nothing less than feeling their unity with all the cosmos will bring the happiness they are searching for. They misplace it and mistakenly think attainment of some external status or material thing will bring them enduring happiness. The heart opening and staying open is what brings enduring happiness because you awaken to your real identity and purpose as a co-creator. You remember that you are a part of something bigger, that you are eternal energy, that you belong and are never alone, and that you are deeply loved.

How do we open our hearts? How can we realize and find this happiness within us? How do we move towards enlightenment?

All I know is my own experience. I am no master. I am not enlightened, but I have had a few glimpses of it.

I noticed 5 actions that led to my awakenings: being passionate, surrendering, deep breathing, exploring Yoga, and reading spiritual encouragement from masters.

BE PASSIONATE

When I first set out for answers, I was extremely passionate. I feel like this was the key that opened the door to my amazing experiences. I was highly active in my seeking. I was enthusiastic and excited. I was all-in. Nothing else mattered. As Ramakrishna, a 19th century Indian mystic and yogi, once said,

> "Do not seek illumination unless you seek it as a man whose hair is on fire seeks a pond."

This level of engagement is crucial not only if you want to discover the truth of what you are, but for living a happy life in general. Your heart, body, and mind must be fully aligned and thrilled to do what you do.

Follow your gut. Follow your excitement. Follow your bliss. Follow your passion. Follow your heart. Following you heart leads to the opening of your heart. The opening of your heart leads to enlightenment. Enlightenment leads to ultimate happiness.

Do what makes you feel the most alive. Use your emotions as a gauge. If you are unhappy, change something in your life. That which excites you is your compass. It is the way the universe leads you to the path you were born to take.

If you want enlightenment and experiences of higher perceptions and energies, you must be all-in: all your heart, body, mind, and soul. You must be ablaze with enthusiastic wonder of the mystery of it all.

This life experience on earth is pretty awesome. It is an adventure. Get stoked! What you put out, is what you get back. Give all your passion, all your heart, and All will give all of its glory back to you.

SURRENDER

Paradoxically, what was necessary for my heart and third eye to open was both active seeking and complete surrender. These opposites work together. After searching and searching, I needed to completely let go in order to receive the grace of divine revelation. Both the reaching for it, then letting it go are required, a balance of both.

Surrender is important.

It may be frightening initially to surrender because it is taking a giant leap of faith. It is diving headfirst off a cliff into the unknown. It is letting go of the ego's tight grip and false sense of control. It is surrendering all that is familiar, and all of what you think keeps you safe. When we surrender, we let all the walls fall that we have built up out of fear.

Surrender allows us to see that we are already one with everything. We are already loved fully by the energy of the universe. We are already spiritual and connected. We have but gotten in our own way. Surrendering gets ourselves out of our own way.

The personality may think that if it is not in control of every detail logically like it has been, then everything would fall apart. Turns out quite the opposite happens. Let go and everything falls into place. Things work out perfectly and everything becomes synchronized with your state of being. Life becomes a fantasy and a dream.

The ego or personality self is not bad. It is what allows us to experience life on this planet, as an individual, as a focused reality of manifestation. It only becomes a hindrance to realizing the truth when it takes on more jobs than it is designed to do, and when it thinks it is all alone. Then it operates from fear. "It is all up to me to keep me safe and to figure everything out that needs to happen. I am on my own."

Surrendering this mindset allows the personality to feel and realize that it is not alone. The higher self, the True Self, the One in all things, loves it and wants to help, but it cannot unless the ego loosens its tight grip.

In my experiences, I did not do anything. I surrendered. The grander presence within me did the work. The energy filled me and opened me and gave me a new perception of a new world.

What we surrender to is the silence, the love, and the will of the One in the heart. When we surrender, we feel like a child again that is taken care of and loved by the One.

Letting go may be emotional. It may feel like a breakdown. All my experiences have been so. All my profound episodes of the heart and light eye opening are initiated when I begin to cry. Strong emotion is important. Emotions are energy in motion: e-motion. In today's culture, we are too judgmental towards certain emotions, especially those that bring tears, and especially among men.

Crying is important and misunderstood. Based on my own experiences, we should never suppress our tears. With them may come the most magnificent experience of an individual's entire life. Mine have. The mental, physical, and emotional release they provide compares to nothing else. The catharsis not only heals but awakens the omnipotent, omniscient, omnipresent True Self within. Heaven is revealed as here and now on the earth. So never hold them back. Trust and surrender.

The release of belief systems that no longer serve you might be necessary, and it might feel like a breakdown because it is a breakdown: a breaking down of limiting perceptions, habits, and thought patterns that have blocked you from your bliss that is available to you always here and now.

So, welcome the rise of emotion. Welcome the tears. Do not fight them. They bring release. They clear the way for love to be received unimpeded. They allow for rebirth into a life where love is recognized and acknowledged as the motivational force in everything, including you.

The personality self, the character, the ego, at times thinks it must achieve and work and put in the time to gain some key. Only when I let go of all such thinking did it open me to the perception of the love in all things. Only when I allowed the divine love to be received did I enter the true state; only when I welcomed the rising emotion, the, at first, panic and anxiety, then the overwhelming, melting love; only when I surrendered and welcomed the breakdown.

BREATHE DEEPLY

The precursor to my heart openings and my third eye opening was surrender, which always led to me sobbing.

As I mentioned earlier, I realized that I can willfully reach a higher state of being by doing a pattern of deep breathing that resembles the breathing pattern that naturally occurs when sobbing.

Deep breathing is a powerful tool to open the heart, and I highly recommend it. It is also remarkably effective in changing your mood if you are upset or sad. I have found that it is the quickest and easiest technique to change my state of mind and being.

First of all, it is always available. We are all breathing all the time. All you need to do is become conscious of it and breathe deeper.

Secondly, you can do it anywhere without making a scene. In other words, you do not need to sit cross legged, close your eyes, and loudly chant OM. In line at the grocery? You can do it. Listening to someone at work judge or complain about another coworker? You can do it. You can do it anywhere.

Lastly, it works without even having to think or visualize. Many tools are mental and require a change in the thought process and inner dialogue. With breathing, you just do it, and it cleans and quiets the mind automatically. This is what I love most about it.

In my experience, all I need is to take a few, 5 to 10, deep belly-filling breaths, and I instantly feel calmer, more peaceful, and better in general. When you do a few more deep breaths, you may find that you suddenly do not know why you were upset or sad in the first place. I have found, after taking 20 to 30 deep breaths, my mind is wiped clean, and I am in awe that I was ever feeling down. It is like it restarts my brain and stops all previous processes that were only slowing it down.

What I mean by breathing deeply is this: when you inhale, you first expand the belly, doing what is called a diaphragmatic breath, bringing air to the bottom of the lungs. Then, you expand the chest to full compacity, the upper part of the lungs. The two combined is called Yogic breathing. The idea is to fill the lungs as much as comfortably possible, then relax and exhale. Repeat. That's it.

Breathe! In my opinion, no other technique is as powerful or transformative.

There are many different methods and schools that teach deep breathing techniques. I have tried most of them and they are all effective. Some force the air out on the exhale. Some insist on breathing through the mouth, others the nose. Some change the pace throughout the practice. Find whichever one is best for you, or just experiment and do your own. It is just breathing. Keep it simple because it is simple. I recommend doing whatever technique you like best as a daily practice. If you meditate, I recommend doing it before meditation.

Deep breathing is a huge aspect of Yoga, called pranayama…

EXPLORE YOGA

> "To the question whether man can here and now attain the supreme state of Bliss, the answer in Yoga is yes."
> –Sir John Woodroffe, *The Serpent Power*

I was first led to Yoga by my visions of Kundalini, and later my interest in it grew even more because of my third eye experience. I have found the third eye subtly mentioned in several different belief systems, but none explore it as deeply and openly as Yoga.

Yoga has become immensely popular, but what we today see, and call Yoga, is only a small portion of the original, ancient practice.

When you hear the word Yoga, what comes to mind? Most likely a studio with a mirrored wall and comfortable, stretchy pants. However, its original, intended purpose was not superb flexibility and a killer bod but realized union with the cosmos, a.k.a. enlightenment. The word Yoga literally means union.

The physical postures that have become so popular, called asanas, are only one of the eight limbs of Yoga. Pranayama is another. Combined with the other six, which are yamas (moral conduct or restraints), niyamas (self-conduct or observances), pratyahara (turning the mind inwards), dharana (concentration), dhyana (meditation), and samadhi (higher states of consciousness or enlightenment), Yoga serves as a system of mental and physical practices and conducts to lead an individual to a direct realization of their oneness with all of creation and its Creator.

I believe that the resurgence of Yoga worldwide is no coincidence. Yes, the asanas portion of Yoga is what is most popular in the west, and it is just a small portion of Yoga, but Yoga is still growing and the, even if shallow at first, introduction of just the asanas will lead people to explore Yoga more deeply. It is growing popularity and spreading for a reason. It is a systematic approach, developed thousands of years ago, for an individual to reach feasible enlightenment. Its philosophies are all true and they work. You do not have to believe they do. If you don't, then they won't. I wouldn't necessarily either if it wasn't for my own experiences. Hence this book. This testimony is meant to expand your beliefs of what is possible and to encourage you to explore, for yourself, your Self.

In my opinion, Yoga is the best introduction to spirituality and overall approach and methodology of exploring Spirit because it emphasizes the gaining of wisdom through direct experience. It acknowledges that the infinite, universal Self is within the individual, and therefore affirms the individual to be the best place of exploration. It has tools for realizing and mastering all aspects of yourself: your body, mind, emotions, energy, and consciousness. It provides a road map to the inner world. It is a complete system for enlightenment.

I will not go into details about Yoga. There are plenty of other books for that, and I whole heartedly recommend the exploration of them.

Check out Yoga if you haven't already. It may change your life like it has changed millions of others'.

READ SPIRITUAL ENCOURAGEMENT FROM MASTERS

What tremendously helped me stay on the path and remain determined to reach a spiritual awakening was advice and encouragement from masters. Reading books such as The Upanishads, The Gospel of Thomas, The Tao-te Ching, The Bhagavad Gita, the Yogasutras, and a handful of modern channeled texts, all confirmed my growing convictions, and thereby motivated me to keep looking. They imparted truths about what we are that I did not find in school. They gave me a sneak peek into what is possible for humankind. They sparked my sense of wonder and excitement. Whenever my enthusiasm was waning, I would turn to them to reignite my passion for the search of self-realization.

I share some of the wisdom that I found in these books in Part 2.

Reading words from masters and channeled guides reminds us of long forgotten truths and helps us realign to the Source of those truths within us. They help us remember what we are.

These 5 things are what led to my profound experiences. I share them in hopes that they will assist you in your inner search.

If these openings can happen to me, they can happen to you. They can happen to everyone.

I wish you happy seeking.

Enough… Rise

"He who seeks will find, and he who knocks will be let in."
–Jesus, Gospel of Thomas, *The Nag Hammadi Library*

I had a dream recently. I was walking through an old, rundown house. I entered a room and suddenly knew that I had been there before as a young child. On the far wall, there was written in big letters, "Enough… Rise." Seeing this sent electricity through my body. It was a weird feeling of something familiar yet long forgotten. I knew that I was the one who had written it as a child, and that I had written it specifically for my future self to read. As a child I knew that I would need a reminder when I was an adult. I woke up with goosebumps.

Enough tinkering with assumptions and thoughts. Rise to the heart's level of knowing.

Enough fear. Rise to love.

It is time to see what we are and are capable of. It is time to remember that the life in us all is the love-intelligence that created, that creates, and that *is* everything.

The heart can open wide and feel, and the third eye can open wide and see, paradise on earth.

There is an astonishing life-force that is here for us, that cares for us, that *is* us.

It wants to be received. It wants us to open and allow it in. It wants to be felt and shared.

The truth of what we are is so humbling.

I was nothing in those moments of opening, yet I was everything.

I, the self I usually identify myself with, the personality self, the character, was nothing. It was just a window through which the mystery radiated, through which the mystery was aware of itself. The mystery is what I really am.

I do nothing. This small self that has a name, that acts a certain way, that others perceive as a persona, does not move the brilliant mystery through the heart, mind, and body.

The mystery itself, the True Self that we are, it knocks at the heart and steps in. It does the work. It brings the epiphany. It spreads the healing peace. It opens the heart and third eye and reveals itself as the truth in all things, reveals itself as the identity of everything.

After my third eye opened, it made sense why I never felt fully myself around others. The personality and character we perform is not what we really are. What we really are is this mystery.

As a species, we have not known what we truly are for so long. Only a few have woken up and remembered in our history. A few have realized and have pointed the way. The majority have forgotten.

Enlightenment is possible. I am not enlightened, but I have seen that it is possible, and it is at first unbelievable, because it is so beyond what we have been taught, so fantastic and infinite.

Seeing our true potential changes everything. It makes one realize that a peaceful and paradisal life on earth is totally possible.

I believe the next step in human evolution is from people operating from individual mindsets to operating from unity consciousness. No longer are we in fear and all thinking that we are separate, alone, competing and fending for ourselves, but are One and operate together as One for the benefit of all.

We can ascend in awareness and see that each and all are fountainheads for the omnipotent, omniscient, and omnipresent love-light, and that the rise towards more love, bliss, and wisdom is endless and eventually certain for everyone. This is our evolution towards the stars.

Does this sound too good to be true? Fact is stranger than fiction. We know an infinitesimal amount about our infinite nature. The fact is we are conduits for the light of the universe, wired for Source's sensuous lightening, circuits for Creator's electric love-power. Strange indeed, for the fact is we are God, dancing in a dream of diversity. Our bodies have the capacity to resonate and amplify the frequency of the Maker of the Stars. They were designed to do so and are meant to do so. The fact is you are eternal and have a heart that houses the ancient wisdom of all the ages. You have a beacon of shimmering, celestial light in the center of your head, a fantastic eye that sees the One spark that started it all in every point of all space.

Yes, strange.

Strange indeed, for we are meant to shine.

The old stories of yogis, saints, gurus, mystics, wizards, witches, sages, and monks performing unbelievable, reality-bending feats, healing the sick, receiving epiphanies and visions from the divine, do not all belong simply in the misty past, in folk tales and legends. These things are possible for modern woman and man. It is time to remember what is possible.

The solution to humans' current problems is us turning towards consciousness. The intelligence within us is the next frontier. Tapping into our own connection to the universe and its creative power is what will heal what needs to be healed, what will transform what needs to be transformed. The planet reflects the consciousness of everyone on it. Change the consciousness, and you change the world.

Love is the Creator, love is in all things, love is the energy and power in every atom, love is the answer, love is the Source, love is the foundational vibration, love is our identity, love is our True Self. Align with it, allow it to be expressed and received and flowed through the body, and the miraculous transformation of your perceptions will happen instantly.

To put this practically, acknowledge every other being, animal, and object you encounter as the Creator, as the same light and Source as you, as the consciousness that is in everything else, as the mysterious and wonderful love power that created all of this, as the face of your dearest friend, and you will open your mind to the cosmic mind.

You will receive the consciousness of God.

You will receive the love of the universe.

You will open to your true inheritance.

You will see earth and all on it as it truly is: a paradise inhabited by glowing angels, who have simply forgotten what they are. The will of the whole, the action that is best for all, will work and express through you, and all doors of perception will open. Everything will appear as light, as energy, not only as physical matter but as wisps of fantastic love-light. The dreamlike nature of reality will be obvious, and you will laugh at the lightness of being. It is all a fantasy we ourselves create.

It is really all about moving into the heart and operating from the heart.

I find that some people, trying to be spiritual, get caught up in theories, metaphysical terms, rituals, or their tools, and forget that all that really matters is to respect, acknowledge, and love each other. The tools are all well and good. They can help. But the tools should not be confused with the goal they help one reach. Obsession with methods and philosophies tends to complicate. The goal is simple. It is to see the One in all things and to act accordingly. The goal is to unconditionally love all and thereby become a conduit for the love in all.

Move into the heart and remember what you are.

You are loved. You are loved. You are loved.

You are love.

Our True Self, when allowed to be received and expressed, will enter and unveil paradise on earth. It has always been here. Allow yourself to feel this love from the Spirit in all things. Allow yourself to be taken care of because you are. Let go of logically needing to know what will happen and how it will happen. It is more of an adventure that way anyway. You were not designed to take on all the burdens yourself. You have backup from True Self, from your Higher Self, from Spirit, from Creator, from the love-light in all things. Allow yourself to be aided by it. Allow it to guide you. How? Move into the heart. Be still and listen.

The goal is to become receptive and aware of the love-light that you are and that you are in, here and now and always. It is not a specific place, but a state of consciousness, a state of being, an awareness of God in all things, an expression of unconditional love, a resonance with the frequency of the foundational love-light that is everything. You are in the kingdom already but may not see it nor experience it. To experience it, love. If someone is mean or upsets you, forgive and love more. Everyone is coming from where they are at, and that is OK. Welcome to earth.

When you love you become open for business and the energy of the cosmos flows through you and out to express on earth. Earth then supports you and entrusts herself to you because you become the embodiment of her true love. You are humming in tune with the melody of the earth and stars, vibrating at the same pitch of the Creator, being reborn as the child of light you are. You become aligned with the force that creates everything and is everything and enter a new world that is here and now.

The experience of my third eye forever changed my life. No other endeavor but to pursue this state of being, establish it fully within myself, share it with others, and help it become realized, makes any sense anymore.

At times I forget and get side-tracked and look outside of myself for fulfillment from material things or physical pleasures, but I always eventually snap out of it and remember what is in store for us. Nothing is as fulfilling as having this expanded consciousness, this cosmic energy, this universal love-light, open your heart and head and pour through. When someone else experiences it, I guarantee it will change everything for them too.

The fact that this state of being is possible here and now has giant implications. In the pursuit of happiness, this should be the goal, because, as mentioned before, the pursuit of enlightenment is the pursuit of *true* happiness.

Remembering and experiencing firsthand that you are the same energy that created the universe, the same energy in everything and everyone, brings ultimate happiness. You realize that you are not alone but are an integral part of the great team that is us all. Not only that, it brings peace. With peace comes the ending of fear. Fear and the belief of the separation of mankind from Creator are the cause of all the world's current problems. One minute of this experience would lead a person to deeply know that every other person essentially is them, that they are the same thing, and that there is nothing to fear.

The third eye is real. Hear this and remember. Do not stop your quest for spiritual growth. Do not stop your search for the expansion of consciousness. It is possible. In your heart is the love-light of the world.

We are the bridges, the conduits, the channels, the great expressers of the light. Through us is how Creator expresses and experiences life. Let us open and remember.

It has been my intention to acknowledge and remind you of your True Self. You know what you are but have simply forgotten. Deep down, you know that you are one with the stars. Deep within you, you know the Creator of all the cosmos beats your heart. You are one with the One life in all things, and you know this. The mind has just gone on a little tangent. It has dreamed up a play of separation, has formulated drama and plot, has cast characters, made villains and heroes, crafted props and costumes, and has set the scene for a grand performance. And oh, what a grand performance it has been. Our planet has been the playhouse for airy comedies and muggy tragedies, full of actors busily playing along with the pretend. At times, the players forget they are playing, so vivid the performance is, so engrossing and moving. They get wrapped up in the drama, play on, uphold the act, and forget. They forget that they write the script, take on the character, establish the plot, and decorate the stage… We forget.

Sleepy dreamers now awake. Awake and see that you dream. I come to gently rock you out of drowsy slumber, to whisper an invitation to join the welcoming of a new dawn on earth.

Arise and behold, you create all of this fantasy.

Arise and behold, you are the beloved.

Arise and behold, you are the identity and mystery of the universe.

Open and see. Heaven is here and now. It is the fire in your heart, the flame ablaze in every brother, sister, mountain, sea, river, tree, plant, animal, molecule, cell, atom—every speck of all space.

Open your eye, your head, and your heart, and see your brother and sister, see mankind, see your family. Open and see the light. Awake and behold, you are home. You never left.

Enlightenment is possible. Do not stop your quest for it. As you rise, you set the example for others and help them see what is possible. Your high vibration will become contagious and spread. As you open more and more, you help everyone open. They see it is possible by your example and seek to do it themselves.

We rise better altogether.

The world needs you.

Enough… Rise.

PART 2:

9 SPIRITUAL TRUTHS

There are 9 main spiritual truths that the world's religious, spiritual, and channeled texts all share. These 9 ring true to my own personal experiences. These have aided me in times of doubt, in times of questioning my own profound openings. They have served as my personal bible. I go to them troubled, read, and then sigh with relief, "Oh yes, of course." I hope they may help you like they have helped me.

1: The One is the All, the All are the One

"A human being is part of the whole, called by us 'universe'—a part limited in time and space. He experiences himself, his thoughts and feelings as something separate from the rest—a kind of optical delusion of consciousness."
–Albert Einstein

The World Redeemer

"Play young child, the first born bright
Know ye not you are a child of light?
Let go, be free
You are meant to be happy
There is never any reason to fear
I AM forever present, I AM always near
It's not possible to be truly lost
Never would light gamble at such a cost
Dreams at times may be a maze
with too thick a musty haze
but do not forget the Inner Dreamer
the Light of the world and the One-Self Seer
For Love, the Light of lights, the Holy Flame
beats your heart, and orchestrates the entire game

"Love encompasses all
from the babies that cry, to the worms that crawl

The wheel I make from head to tail
Doth loop it all, from serpent to whale
Every line of symmetry I circuit through
for I AM the creator of this planet of green and blue
Surrender unto me, for I AM the self in thee
the self in he, the self in she,
the self in mountain and in tree
A myriad of dreams, but One Dreamer
Look to the Light in the Heart, to the World Redeemer"

I am amazed by this grace
A dreaming dragon suddenly appeared on the inner wall of my own face
Its radiant fantasy, is more real than reality
Others proclaim insanity, but it perfects my mentality
So grand, so mystical, so giving and wise
Even through its closed lids I feel its piercing eyes
Its divinity glows, as if to say:
"Surrender unto me, I AM the way
I AM all your scenery
The self in thee, the self in she, the self in everything you see
The self in mountain and in tree
A myriad of dreams but One Dreamer
Look to the Light in the Heart, to the World Redeemer

"Cease your fidgeting, relax in my arms
Breathe deep and fan this fire; no need to be alarmed
This is your true heaven and home, this Holy Heart Flame
This life primordial, this True Self within, forever the same
I AM Light and you are my daughter and son
but this difference is illusion, we are One
A myriad of dreams but One Dreamer
I AM the Light in the Heart; I AM the World Redeemer"

After my third eye experience, it suddenly made sense of what mystics, gurus, sages, shamans, poets, and saints have been saying all along: the

One in us is the One in all. This life, love, and light in the heart, that is our identity, is the life, love, and light in all things. Have I said this before? Do I keep repeating myself? Yes! And I'll say it again and again! We are not separate from Creator, God, Goddess, Consciousness, Life Energy, the Field, the Source, the One, the Universe, Brahman, Atman, the Tao, the Light, the Love-Light, Spirit, the Great Spirit, the Force, the Infinite, the Eternal, the Father, the Mother, the True Self, whatever you wish to call it. It doesn't matter what name you use, as long as you understand that it is One, it is everything, and it is what you really are. It is your real self. To realize it in yourself and in everything else, *see* it in everything and acknowledge it.

> "See the Self in all."
> –Kena Upanishad, *The Upanishads*, trans. Eknath Easwaran[12]

> "I am the light that is over all things. I am all: from me all has come forth and to me all has reached. Split a piece of wood, I am there. Lift up the stone, and you will find me there."
> –Jesus, Gospel of Thomas, *The Nag Hammadi Library*

> "The Soul (Ātman), indeed, is below. The Soul is above. The Soul is to the west. The Soul is to the east. The Soul is to the south. The Soul is to the north. The Soul, indeed, is this whole world."
> –Chandogya Upanishad 7.25.2, *The Thirteen Principal Upanishads* trans. Robert Ernest Hume

> "Behold the One in all things; it is the second that leads you astray."
> –Kabir

> "When a man sees All in all, then a man stands beyond mere understanding."–Meister Eckhart

---

[12]From The Upanishads, translated by Eknath Easwaran, founder of the Blue Mountain Center of Meditation, copyright 1987, 2007; reprinted by permission of Nilgiri Press, P. O. Box 256, Tomales, Ca 94971, www.easwaran.org.

"You can not see the seer of seeing. You can not hear the hearer of hearing. You can not think the thinker of thinking. You can not understand the understander of understanding. He is your soul, which is in all things. Aught else than Him [or, than this] is wretched."
–Brhadaranyaka Upanishad 3.4.2, *The Thirteen Principal Upanishads* trans. Robert Ernest Hume

"Withersoever ye turn, these is the presence of Allah."
–Mohammad, Quran 2:115, *Sacred Books of the East*

"All things are Buddha-things."
–Vajracchedika ("The Diamond Cutter") *Sacred Books of the East*

"Remember, that there is only One Thing in the Universe, that is Permanent, Real, Eternal, and That is the 'I AM presence,' of God in you, which is the owner, the creator, the intelligence governing all manifested form. Then to know that you are that 'Presence' that 'I AM' Presence, places you, beloved student, independent of all outer manifestation."
–Godfre Ray King, *The I AM Discourses*

"Those who possess this wisdom have equal regard for all. They see the same Self in a spiritual aspirant, and an outcaste, in an elephant, a cow, and a dog. Such people have mastered life. With even mind they rest in Brahman, who is perfect and is everywhere the same."
–Krishna, *Bhagavad-Gita*, trans. Eknath Easwaran[13]

"All things are one … there is no polarity, no right or wrong, no disharmony, but only identity. All is one, and that one is love/light, light/love, the infinite Creator."
–The Law of One, Book 1

---

13 From The Bhagavad Gita, translated by Eknath Easwaran, founder of the Blue Mountain Center of Meditation, copyright 1985, 2007; reprinted by permission of Nilgiri Press, P. O. Box 256, Tomales, CA 94971, www.easwaran.org.

"God is the source. God is the great source. God is the frequency and the energy that joyfully permeates all matter. God is everything. God is everything. God is everything. And we say this with joy."
–Paul Selig, *I Am the Word* [14]

"The first change that should occur in the behavior of a mortal when his mind begins to mirror God is to perceive his *identity* with other human beings. The perception of this unity, in turn, should fill him with an ardent desire to make them sharers of his own sublime experience and overflowing happiness."
–Gopi Krishna, *Living with Kundalini: The autobiography of Gopi Krishna*

"That which is diversity has been misconceived from the personal, or external viewpoint, to be separation. The great work for each soul is to lift the personal viewpoint to such great heights in consciousness that it becomes one with the whole."
–Baird T. Spalding, *Life and Teaching of the Masters of the Far East*

"He really sees who sees the highest lord standing equal among all creatures, undecaying amid destruction."
–Krishna, *Bhagavad-Gita,* trans. Barbara Stoler Miller

"There is something, amorphous and complete, that was born before Heaven and Earth. Obscure, oh, it stands alone, unchanged. It operates everywhere but is free from danger, thus we may consider it the mother of all under Heaven."
–Lao-Tzu, *Tao-te Ching*, trans. Richard John Lynn

---

[14] Excerpt(s) from I AM THE WORD: A GUIDE TO THE CONSCIOUSNESS OF MAN'S SELF IN A TRANSITIONING TIME by Paul Selig, copyright © 2010 by Paul Selig. Used by permission of TarcherPerigee, an imprint of the Penguin Publishing Group, a division of Penguin Random House LLC . All rights reserved.

"Although the Supersoul appears to be divided among beings, He is never divided. He is situated as one. He is the source of light in all luminous objects. He is beyond the darkness of matter and is un-manifested. He is knowledge, and he is the goal of knowledge. He is situated in everyone's heart."
–Krishna, *Bhagavad-Gita, As it is*, trans. A.C. Bhaktivedanta Swami Prabhupada

"I am you and you are me, and where you are, there I am. I am sown in all things, and when you gather me, it is you, yourself, whom you gather."
–Jesus, Gospel of Eve, *The Lost Books of the Bible and the forgotten books of Eden*

"It shall be understood that any portion, no matter how small, of any density or illusory pattern contains, as in a holographic picture, the one Creator which is infinity. Thus all begins and ends in mystery."
–*The Law of One, Book 1*

"You are the Self, the infinite Being, the pure unchanging consciousness, which pervades everything."
–Shankara

"The Self is the witness, all-pervading, perfect, free, one, consciousness, actionless, not attached to any object, desireless, ever tranquil. It appears through illusion as the world."
–Ashtavakra Gita

"The infinite dwelling of the Infinite Being is everywhere: in earth, water, sky, and air... He who is within is without. I see Him and none else."
–Kabir

"Learn to look with an equal eye upon all beings, seeing the one Self in all."
–Srimad Bhagavatam

"The world is no more than the Beloved's single face. In the desire of the One to know its own beauty, we exist."
–Ghalib

"There is no other material cause of the universe than Brahman; this whole world is in fact Brahman and nothing else."
–Shankara

"Nay, I would rather say, not that God contains all things, but that, to speak the full truth, God is all things."
–Hermes Trismegistus

"Talk as much philosophy as you please, worship as many gods as you like, observe all ceremonies, sing devoted praises to any number of divine beings –liberation never comes, even at the end of a hundred aeons, without the realization of the oneness of the self."
–Shankara

2: The Golden Rule

What is enlightenment? Enlightenment is fully remembering and experiencing in every moment the truth that the One is the all, the all are the One, and that you are one with this One.

So, enlightenment is experiencing and seeing firsthand, in every moment, the One in all things, feeling and knowing deeply that the One in all things is the same One within you, and therefore *acting accordingly.*

Acting accordingly is doing the will of the One, and in so doing, becoming a conduit for the power of the One. And by being a conduit, the individual then receives a higher perception, knowledge, and power.

What is the will of the One?

It can be summed up by the golden rule: treat others as you would like to be treated. Pretty simple, yet powerful. Why? Because acting this way acknowledges the truth of unity.

The golden rule is found in every major religion. It is the main theme of them all, and it sums up all the lengthy spiritual texts from all over the globe in one sentence.

> "Do to others as you would have them do to you. … Love your enemies, do good, and lend, expecting nothing in return. Your reward will be great, and you will be children of the Most High."
> –Jesus, Luke 6:31,35, *The New Oxford Annotated Bible*

> "This is the sum of duty: do naught unto others which would cause you pain if done to you."
> –Hinduism, *Mahabharata* 5: 1517

"Hurt not others in ways that you yourself would find hurtful."
–Buddhism, *Udana-Varga* 5:18

"Thou shalt Love thy neighbor as thyself."
–Judaism, *Leviticus* 19:18

"Whatever is disagreeable to yourself, do not do unto others."
–Zoroastrianism, *Shast-na-shayast* 13:29

"One should always treat others as they themselves wish to be treated."
–Hinduism, *Hitopadesa*

"Surely it is the maxim of loving kindness: Do not do unto others what you would not have them do unto you."
–Confucianism, *Analects* 15:23

"Regard your neighbor's gain as your own gain and your neighbor's loss as your own loss."
–Taoism, *T'ai Shang Kan Ying P'ien*

"That nature alone is good which refrains from doing unto another whatsoever is not good for itself."
–Zoroastrainism, *Dadistan-I-dinik* 94:5

"No one of you is a believer until he desires for his brother that which he desires for himself."
–Islam, *Sunnah*

"What is hateful to you, do not to your fellowman. That is the entire law; all the rest is commentary."
–Judaism, *Talmud*, Shabbat 31a

"Love your brother like your soul, guard him like the pupil of your eye."
–Jesus, Gospel of Thomas, *The Nag Hammadi Library*

"The Man of Calling has no heart of his own. He makes the people's heart his own heart. 'To the good I am good; to the non good I am also good; for life is goodness."
–Lao-Tzu, *Tao-te Ching*, trans. Richard Wilhelm

"The Great Cosmic Law is unerring. We cannot receive without giving, and we cannot give without receiving. Thus, the Great Balance of Life is maintained."
–Godfre Ray King, *Unveiled Mysteries*

"When you have seen your brothers as yourself you will be released."
–*A Course in Miracles* T-13.VIII.8:1.[15]

"What you do not want done unto you, do not feel that it is done unto you or another. This is the whole law of a full and happy life. Everything else is commentary."
–Neville Goddard, *Feeling is the Secret*

"Act in such a way that you treat humanity, whether in your own person or in the person of any other, never merely as a means to an end, but always at the same time as an end."
–Immanuel Kant, *Grounding for the Metaphysics of Morals*

"So in everything, do unto others what you would have them do to you, for this sums up the Law and the Prophets."
–Jesus, Matthew 7:12, *The New Oxford Annotated Bible*

---

[15] From *A Course in Miracles*, copyright ©1992, 1999, 2007 by the Foundation for Inner Peace, P.O. Box 598, Mill Valley, CA 94942-0589, www.acim.org and info@acim.org, used with permission.

"Do not judge, so that you may not be judged. For with the judgment you make you will be judged, and the measure you give will be the measure you get."
–Jesus, Matthew 7:1-2, *The New Oxford Annotated Bible*

"Therefore: by your own person judge the person of the other. … How do I know the nature of the world? Just through this."
–Lao-Tzu, *Tao-te Ching*, trans. Richard Wilhelm

3: Know Thyself

"Tat tvam asi (Thou art that)." –The Upanishads

"The travesty of mankind is that you think you are not divine."
–Paul Selig, *The Book of Freedom*

You are the One

Our purpose here is to recall the inner spark
While sitting surrounded by the dark
To remember and to shine, shine bright
Even while immersed in the veil of the night
What a privilege, what an exciting goal
To remember and reveal that which is already whole
Look homeward now angel and melt from the truth
And remember what your heart sang while in youth
It sings on, just be silent and still
Listen to the heart and in your body a light will fill
The light of the world, the light of lights
The light of the cosmos, the holy light bright
All will open up, as vast as the sky
And you will pierce through the dream, and see through the light eye
Our very own brain
All of the cosmos contains
Within thy heart
Is the creator from the start

Be silent be still
Breathe deep and keep
Calm the wild will
Behold what you really are
More magnificent than a blazing star
No need to fret anymore
You are the One you have been waiting for

Throughout time masters, gurus, saints, prophets, poets, and philosophers have all given the crucial advice to know thyself. Know what you are, how you operate, and you will see that the life-energy in you is the life-energy in the seed, the animal, the plant, the river, and the earth, and that this life-energy is bursting with bliss.

To realize your true state of being, to open the heart and head, to experience your unity with the earth and the cosmos, look within. Look within your own heart, and you shall find this love-light. You shall realize the bliss that has always been there. You shall discover the great mysteries of the universe, for your consciousness is one with the consciousness that created, and that *is*, the universe.

> "You are the light of the world. A city on a hill cannot be hidden. Neither do people light a lamp and put it under a bowl. Instead they put it on its stand, and it gives light to everyone in the house. In the same way, let your light shine before men."
> –Jesus, Matthew 5:14-16, *The New Oxford Annotated Bible*

> "Seek not abroad, turn back into thyself, for in the inner man dwells the truth."
> –St. Augustine

> "Self-realization is God-realization."
> –*Emmanuel's Book: A Manual for Living Comfortably in the Cosmos*[16]

[16] Excerpt(s) from EMMANUEL'S BOOK: A MANUAL FOR LIVING COMFORTABLY IN THE COSMOS compiled by Pat Rodegast and Judith Stanton,

"The 'I AM' in you created everything in the universe."
–Godfre Ray King, *The I AM Discourses*

"Of all knowledge the wise and good seek most to know themselves."
–William Shakespeare

"Seek not outside yourself … For all your pain comes simply from a futile search of what you want, insisting where it must be found. … Be you glad that you are told where happiness abides, and seek no longer elsewhere. You will fail. But it is given you to know the truth and not to seek for it outside yourself."
–A Course in Miracles, T-29.VII.1:7,10-12.

"You are not only in eternity. You are eternity. You are not only with God. You are God."
–Emmanuel's Book III: What is an Angel doing here?

"One who knows everything but lacks in oneself lacks in everything."
–Jesus, Gospel of Thomas, *The Nag Hammadi Library*

"The heavens and the earth will be rolled up in your presence. And the one who lives from the Living One will not see death. … Whoever finds himself is superior to the world."
–Jesus, Gospel of Thomas, *The Nag Hammadi Library*

"The further out one goes, the lesser one's knowledge becomes. Therefore, the Man of Calling does not need to go and yet he knows everything."
–Lao-Tzu, *Tao-te Ching*, trans. Richard Wilhelm

"The Way lies at hand yet it is sought afar off; the thing lies in the easy yet it is sought in the difficult."
–Mencius

"Nothing appeared closed to me: because I was the door of everything."
–Odes of Solomon, Ode 17, *The Lost Books of the Bible and the forgotten books of Eden*

"Lo, I am with you always means when you look for God, God is in the look of your eyes, in the thought of looking, nearer to you then yourself or things that have happened to you. There is no need to go outside."
–Rumi, trans. Coleman Barks

"Can there be anything not known to That Who is the One in all? Know One, know all."
–Katha Upanishad 2.1.3, *The Upanishads*, trans. Eknath Easwaran

"Lo, verily, it is the Soul (*Ātman*) that should be seen, that should be hearkened to, that should be thought on, that should be pondered on, O Maitreyī. Lo, verily, with the seeing of, with the hearkening to, with the thinking of, and with the understanding of the Soul, this world—all is known."
–Brhadaranyaka Upanishad 2.4.5, *The Thirteen Principal Upanishads* trans. Robert Ernest Hume

"He who, dwelling in the mind, yet is other than the mind, whom the mind does not know, whose body the mind is, who controls the mind from within—He is your Soul, the Inner Controller, the Immortal."
–Brhadaranyaka Upanishad 3.7.20, *The Thirteen Principal Upanishads* trans. Robert Ernest Hume

"If those who lead you say to you, 'See, the kingdom is in the sky,' then the birds of the sky will precede you. If they say to you, 'It is in the sea,' then the fish will precede you. Rather, the kingdom is inside of you, and it is outside of you. When you come to know yourselves, then you will become known, and you will realize that it is you who are the sons of the living father."
–Jesus, Gospel of Thomas, *The Nag Hammadi Library* (repeated this quote from earlier chapter intentionally to have it side by side with the following quote)

"'You idiot,' said Yājñavalkya, 'that you will think that it could be anywhere else than in ourselves! for if it were anywhere else than in ourselves, the dogs might eat it or the birds might tear it to pieces.'"
–Brhadaranyaka Upanishad 3.9.25, *The Thirteen Principal Upanishads* trans. Robert Ernest Hume

"If a person knew the Soul (*Ātman*), with the thought 'I am he!' with what desire, for love of what, would he cling unto the body? He who has found and has awakened to the Soul that has entered this conglomerate abode—He is the maker of everything, for he is the creator of all; The world is his: indeed, he is the world itself. Verily, while we are here we may know this. If you have known it not, great is the destruction. Those who know this become immortal, but others go only to sorrow. If one perceives Him as the Soul, as God (*deva*), clearly, As the Lord of what has been and of what is to be—One does not shrink away from Him."
–Brhadaranyaka Upanishad 4.4.12-17, *The Thirteen Principal Upanishads* trans. Robert Ernest Hume

"The cosmogonic cycle is presented with astonishing consistency in the sacred writings of all the continents, and it gives to the adventure of the hero a new and interesting turn; for it now appears that the perilous journey was a labor not of attainment but of re-attainment, not discovery but rediscovery.

The godly powers sought and dangerously won are revealed to have been within the heart of the hero all the time."
–Joseph Campbell, *The Hero with a Thousand Faces*

"That which in you sees and hears is not of the earth, but is the Word of God incarnate."
–Manly P. Hall, *The Secret Teachings of all Ages*

"What the undeveloped man seeks is outside; what the advanced man seeks is within himself."
–Confucius, *Analects*

"I know myself now, and I feel within me
A peace above all earthly dignities,
A still and quiet conscience."
–William Shakespeare

"That which you have will save you if you bring it forth from yourselves."
–Jesus, Gospel of Thomas, *The Nag Hammadi Library*

"When a man comes to know that highest brahman, he himself becomes that very brahman."
–Mundaka Upanishad 3.2.9, *The Thirteen Principal Upanishads* trans. Robert Ernest Hume

"I AM that I AM." –Exodus 3:14, *The New Oxford Annotated Bible*

"Be still and know that I AM God."
–Psalm 46:10, *The New Oxford Annotated Bible*

"If you put your soul against this oar with me, the power that made the universe will enter your sinew from a source not outside of your limbs, but from a holy realm that lives in us."
–Rumi, trans. Coleman Barks

"This above all: to thine own self be true,
And it must follow, as the night the day,
Thou canst not then be false to any man."
–William Shakespeare

"We are all Christs and don't realize it."
–Joseph Campbell, *Reflections on the Art of Living*

"And what is the use of knowing many things if, when you have learned the dimensions of heaven and earth, the measure of the seas, the courses of stars, the virtues of plants and stones, the secrets of nature, you still don't know yourself?"
–Petrarch

"Every man is a divinity in disguise, a god playing the fool."
–Ralph Waldo Emerson

"What is here, is found elsewhere. But what is not here, is nowhere else."
–Hinduism, *Mahabharata*

"Man is a microcosm. The world is the macrocosm. There are numberless worlds, each of which is governed by its own Lords, though there is but one great Mother of all whom these Lords themselves worship, placing on their heads the dust of Her feet. In everything there is all that is in anything else. There is thus nothing in the universe which is not in the human body. There is no need to throw one's eyes into the heavens to find God. He is within, being known as the ruler within or inner self. All else is His power as Mind and Matter. Whatever of Mind or Matter exists in the universe exists in some form or matter in the human body."
–Sir John Woodroffe, *The Serpent Power*

"Everything in the universe is within you. Ask all from yourself."
–Rumi, trans. Coleman Barks

"There is an inmost center in us all, where truth abides in fullness."
–Robert Browning

"Look within. Within is the fountain of good."
–Marcus Aurelius

"You who want knowledge, seek the Oneness within. There you will find the clear mirror already waiting."
–Hadewijch

4: Creator is in your Heart

> "Your vision will become clear only when you look into your heart. … Who looks outside, dreams. Who looks inside, awakens."
> –Carl G. Jung

The Sound

the one all around   in every tree and sea found
is the pound of the center   the life giving sound

the thump of the axis   the bump of the pump
pulsates to extremities   then thumps back to pump

and like this it resounds   through all without bounds
the one all around   in every tree and sea found
is the pound of the center   the life giving sound

The heart is the location of the macrocosm within the microcosm, the house of the universal energy within the human body.

The light in the heart is the light in everything.

The heart is the dwelling place of God.

The first opening of my heart prompted my initial search for answers. When it cracks open, it brings a presence of loving intelligence within me. It feels like I am home, taken care of, supported, and unconditionally loved. It feels amazing. The heart experience is beyond the mind's logic. It is beyond the ego. This experience of the heart, of feeling our union with every other creature and all of creation, is the ultimate goal of all spirituality.

Becoming more enlightened is really just moving into and operating from the heart. Then the individual realizes that she or he is already spiritual and so is everything and everyone else.

Moving into the heart does not require new techniques or esoteric jargon or tales of ancient avatars. Breathe deep, go quiet, melt into the heart, allow yourself to receive the love from the universe, and perceive earth like a child again. Use any method that works best for you: meditating, breathing deeply, taking a stroll in nature, praying, painting, dancing, doing a head-stand—whatever works, whatever it takes for you to go lovingly from the head to the heart.

Do that which best moves you gently out of the constant commentary, the individualistic, linguistic, egoic, competitive, survival/fear-based mindset into the heart and into the innocent, quiet now-perception of the love in you and in all things.

The heart is mentioned often in religious texts. The Upanishads, ancient Sanskrit texts considered the core of Hinduism and of Yoga, speak of the importance of the heart repeatedly. In the Bhagavad-Gita, Krishna says he is in the hearts of all men. Jesus placed the treasure that cannot be destroyed within the heart.

Science today is discovering the high level of intelligence and the powerful electromagnetic field of the heart. Physiologically speaking, the heart is a big deal. It's important, obviously. Its beating is what gives us life. Spiritually speaking, the heart is also a very big deal, because the physical and the spiritual are one and the same. The location of the source of life in the human body is the location of our ultimate Source.

Whenever you are in doubt, listen to your heart. This may sound cheesy, but it is advice we hear often because it is good advice. It is crucial advice. Your heart is your inner compass that always points to the truth. Your heart is the physical space where your intimate connection to your True Self is. You want to find God? Look within your own heart.

If I were asked to give spiritual advice but had to give it in one sentence, it would be this:

Surrender to the love, the light, the intelligence, the consciousness, and the will that is in your own heart.

> "As is one's consciousness, so one becomes: that is the eternal secret. ... The mind should be kept in check until it has dissolved into the heart: this is both knowledge and liberation. The rest is just multiplication of books."
> –Maitri Upanishad 4.6, *The Upanishads*, trans. Valerie J. Roebuck

> "He who was born before heat, who before the waters was born, who has seen through living beings—entering the cave of the heart, [one sees] him abiding there."
> –Katha Upanishad 4.6-7, *The Thirteen Principal Upanishads* trans. Robert Ernest Hume

> "This person (*puruṣa*) here in the heart is made of mind, is of the nature of light, is like a little grain of rice, is a grain of barley. This very one is ruler of everything, is lord of everything, governs this whole universe, whatsoever there is."
> –Brhadaranyaka Upanishad 5.6.1, *The Thirteen Principal Upanishads* trans. Robert Ernest Hume

> "If they [i.e. the pupils] should say to him: 'This abode, the small lotus-flower that is here in this city of Brahma, and the small space within that—what is there which should be searched out, which assuredly one should desire to understand?' he should say: 'As far, verily, as this world-space (ayam ākāśa) extends, so far extends the space within the heart. Within it, indeed, are contained both heaven and earth, both fire and wind, both sun and moon, lightning and the stars, both what one possesses here and what one does not possess; everything here is contained within it.'"
> –Chandogya Upanishad 8.1.2-3, *The Thirteen Principal Upanishads* trans. Robert Ernest Hume

"As the innermost Self of all, he dwells within the cavern of the heart. ... The Lord of Love is the one Self of all. ... Realize the Self hidden in the heart, and cut asunder the knot of ignorance here and now. Bright but hidden, the Self dwells in the heart. ... He is the source of love and may be known through love but not through thought. He is the goal of life. Attain this goal! ... Realize him as the One behind the many and stop all vain talk. ... The Self reveals Himself to the one who longs for the Self."
–Mundaka Upanishad, *The Upanishads*, trans. Eknath Easwaran

"You are the supreme Brahman, infinite, yet hidden in the hearts of all creatures. You pervade everything. Realizing you, we attain immortality. ... The Lord of Love, omnipresent, dwelling in the heart of every living creature, all mercy, turns every face to himself. He is the supreme Lord, who through his grace moves us to seek him in our own hearts. He is the light that shines forever. He is the inner Self of all, hidden like a flame in the heart. Only by the stilled mind can he be known. Those who realize him become immortal. He has thousands of heads, thousands of eyes, thousands of feet; he surrounds the cosmos on every side. This infinite being is ever present in the hearts of all."
–Shvetashvatara Upanishad 3.7,11-15, *The Upanishads*, trans. Eknath Easwaran

"I am in everyone's heart as the Supersoul."
–Krishna, *Bhagavad-Gita, As it is*, trans. A.C. Bhaktivedanta Swami Prabhupada

"Therefore, having been born in this transient and forlorn world, give all your love to me. Fill your mind with me, love me, serve me, worship me always. Seeking me in your heart, you will at last be united with me."
–Krishna, *The Bhagavad-Gita*, trans. Eknath Easwaran

"Make purses for yourselves that do not wear out, an unfailing treasure in heaven, where no thief comes near and no moth destroys. For where your treasure is, there your heart will be also."
–Jesus, Luke 12:33-34, *The Holy Bible King James Version*

"If one is to have enlightenment, one must treasure it up from the heart."
–Chen Weiming, Tai Chi master

"The only path that is right for you is the one that is already designed within you. To find this path you have to hear your own heart. ... While the small mind, in its fear, is rigid and controlling, the deeper part of you will begin to whisper the truth of your eternal safety and your Oneness with God. So listen to your heart. This is where your light is and your truth."
–Emmanuel's Book: A Manual for Living Comfortably in the Cosmos

"The greatest wisdom is your own heart."
–Emmanuel's Book III: What is an Angel doing here?

"Knowing that it is the 'Presence of God, I AM' that beats your heart, then you know that your heart is the Voice of God speaking, and as you come to meditate upon the Great Truth: 'I AM the Supreme Intelligent Activity through my mind and heart,' you will bring the True Dependable Divine feeling into your heart."
–Godfre Ray King, *The I AM Discourses*

"Where then shall God be found? Search not in distant skies; in man's own heart he lies."
–Shao Yong

"Why wilt thou go into jungles? What do you hope to find there? Even as the scent dwells within the flower, so God within thine

own heart ever abides. Seek him with earnestness and find Him there."
–Sikhism, as quoted in *Oneness* by Jeffery Moses

"I am the flame that burns in every heart of man, and in the core of every star. … remember all ye existence is pure joy."
–Aleister Crowley, *The Book of the Law*

"The Christ within you is a frequency that is aligned within the heart center and it glows like a flame and it brings to it that vibration and frequency that co-resonates with it. And that which it brings to co-resonance is the Creator."
–Paul Selig, *I Am the Word*

"Now, among the Pueblo Indians in New Mexico I made friends with an interesting fellow who was the chief of religious ceremonies. He confessed to me that they believed all Americans were crazy because they said they thought in the head, whereas the Indians knew that the normal thing was to think in the heart."
–C.G. Jung, *The Psychology of Kundalini Yoga*

"All that is necessary is to look into one's own heart; for what God asks of us is not found at a great distance."
–St. Jerome

5: Become like a Child

> "Except ye become as little children, ye shall not enter the Kingdom of Heaven."
> –Jesus, Gospel of Thomas, *The Nag Hammadi Library*

What does it mean to be like a child? Everyone knows, because everyone once was one or still is one. To be childlike is to be operating less from logic, the intellect, and the ego, and more from the heart. It is to be living more in love and less in fear. As a child you listen to what you came into this world with, more than the spoon-fed knowledge of how to be from society and history. A child doesn't hold back or suppress their expression of joy or love. A child is taken care of. To remember our oneness with the Creator and that we ultimately are always taken care of is to be as a child again.

During my heart openings and eye openings, I feel like a child. There is no thought of yesterday's or tomorrow's troubles, only the innocence of enjoying the body in play and gazing in wonder at the mysterious and beautiful earth around me. And in that mystery, I know I am taken care of and loved deeply by a greater presence within my heart, and within the earth. Mother knocks on the heart, steps in and embraces me, but only when I surrender, let go of acquired knowledge, and become the child that I truly am.

> "Jesus saw infants being suckled. He said to His disciples, 'These infants being suckled are like those who enter the Kingdom.'"
> –The Gospel of Thomas, *The Nag Hammadi Library*

"Once one has access to the mother, through it he can know the child. Once one knows the child, if he again holds onto the mother, as long as he lives, no danger shall befall him."
–Lao-Tzu, *Tao-te Ching*, trans. Richard John Lynn

"Whosoever holds fast to life's completeness is like a newborn infant."
–Lao-Tzu, *Tao-te Ching*, trans. Richard Wilhelm

"'Let the little children come to me; do not stop them; for it is to such as these that the kingdom of God belongs. Truly, I tell you, whoever does not receive the kingdom of God as a little child will never enter it.'"
–Jesus, Mark 10:14-15, *The New Oxford Annotated Bible*

"Yet I have said, whichever one of you comes to be a child will be acquainted with the kingdom and will be superior to John."
–Jesus, Gospel of Thomas, *The Nag Hammadi Library*

"Rely exclusively on your vital force, and become perfectly soft: can you play the infant?"
–Lao-Tzu, *Tao-te-Ching*, trans. Richard John Lynn

"Grown men can learn from very little children for the hearts of little children are pure. Therefore, the Great Spirit may show to them many things which older people miss."
–Black Elk, Native American Medicine Man of Oglala Lakota (Sioux)

"When you disrobe without being ashamed and take up your garments and place them under your feet like little children and tread on them then you will see the Son of the Living One, and you will not be afraid."
–Jesus, Gospel of Thomas, *The Nag Hammadi Library*

"Practice acquiring the consciousness of childhood. Visualize the Divine Child within. … Truly divine love in demonstration is eternal youth. The divine alchemist is within my temple, constantly coining new and beautiful baby cells. The spirit of youth is within my temple—this human form divine, and all is well. … Learn to smile in the sweet way of a child."
–Baird T. Spalding, *Life and Teachings of the Masters of the Far East V.1*

"The great man is he who does not lose his child's heart."
–Mencius

"God said, 'The world is a play, a children's game and you are the children.'"
–Rumi, trans. Coleman Barks

6: Surrender

"Come unto me, for my yoke is easy and my lordship mild, and you will find repose for yourselves."
–Jesus, Gospel of Thomas, *The Nag Hammadi Library*

"It doesn't require work to be as you are. It requires allowance and alignment."
–Paul Selig, *The Book of Truth*[17]

Surrendering initiated all my heart openings and eye openings.

This idea of surrender shows up perpetually in spiritual texts. It instructs us on what to do with all the walls we have constructed around ourselves: surrender all of what you think you know, surrender ideas of what you think you should be or do, let go of the personality or small self's need to control and understand everything, stop trying to logic your way through everything, cease conscious effort, and let go.

Surrender allows us to see that we are already enlightened. We are already one with everything.

"This is a light abounding in full gladness, like coming upon a light in thick darkness, like receiving treasury in poverty. So easy, so free are you, that the weight of the world and the aggravations

[17] Excerpt(s) from THE BOOK OF TRUTH: THE MASTERY TRILOGY: BOOK II by Paul Selig, copyright © 2017 by Paul Selig. Used by permission of TarcherPerigee, an imprint of the Penguin Publishing Group, a division of Penguin Random House LLC . All rights reserved.

of the mind are burdens no longer; your existence is delivered from all limitations. You have become open, light and transparent. You gain an illuminating insight into the deepest nature of things, which appear to you as so many gossamer patterns having no graspable reality! Here is the original face of your being. Here is the straight passage, open and unobstructed. Here is where you surrender all. This is where you gain peace, ease, non-doing and inexpressible delight. All sutras and scriptures are nothing more than communications of this fact. All the sages, ancient and modern, have exhausted their ingenuity and imaginations to no other purpose than to point the way to this!"
–Shih Shuan, *One Song*

"God does not ask anything else of you except that you let yourself go and let God be God in you."
–Meister Eckhart

"This is not the mortal self, the self you see, that is able to do these things. It is a truer deeper self. It is what you know as God, God within me, God the Omnipotent One working through me, that does these things. Of myself, the mortal self, I can do nothing. It is only when I get rid of the outer entirely and let the actual, the I AM, speak and work and let the great Love of God come forth that I can do these things that you have seen. When you let the love of God pour through you to all things, nothing fears you and no harm can befall you."
–Baird T. Spalding, *Life and Teaching of the Masters of the Far East V.1*

"You do not do it. It is done through you. The Divine operates as and through you. You are not pulling the strings on the machine that would enlighten you."
–Paul Selig, *The Book of Mastery*

"The key to the Kingdom has always been you. It always will be. But not at the level of the personality, which is what gets you frustrated. … You do not become the Christ, the Divine Self, the True Self, the Infinite Self, whatever you wish to call it. The Christ becomes you, the Divine as you, the truth as you, love as you in broadcast and expression. The idea of being in form as the Divine Self is age-old, but it has been misunderstood."
–Paul Selig, *The Book of Truth*

"The comprehension of this [the True Self as you and as all things] is not done through the intellect. It cannot be done there. In fact, the intellect will tie it in a knot and a bow and spend the rest of her life trying to untangle it. The True Self knows, the small self thinks. And the comprehension of this teaching must be done in experience."
–Paul Selig, *The Book of Truth*

"The Intelligence that rules the universe is entirely beyond the grasp of our intellect. The disproportion between human intellect and Divine Intelligence can be illustrated by the analogy of the brightly lit specks of dust floating in a state of motion in a shaft of sunlight entering a dark chamber, as compared to the blinding radiance on the surface of the sun."
–Gopi Krishna, *Living with Kundalini: The autobiography of Gopi Krishna*

"He should gradually become tranquil, firmly controlling his understanding; focusing his mind on the self, he should think nothing."
–Krishna, *Bhagavad-Gita*, trans. Barbara Stoler Miller

"As you release, so will you be released. Forget this not, or love will be unable to find you and comfort you."
–A Course in Miracles, T-16.VI.2:4-5.

"In your culture it is thought that the mind must lead, and the heart must follow, suspected of irrationality. I wish to reverse that misconception and to give you back your heart, your soul energy, your spontaneity and love of life. …Thought is a tool to get you to the gate. Then you must leave your tools behind."
–Emmanuel's Book: A Manual for Living Comfortably in the Cosmos

"We, as separate individuals, must not try to think it, but rather permit ourselves to be thought by it."
–Aldous Huxley, *The Perennial Philosophy*

"You ask, how can we know the infinite? I answer, not by reason. It is the office of reason to distinguish and define. The infinite therefore cannot be ranked among its objects. You can only apprehend the infinite by a faculty superior to reason, by entering a state in which you are your finite self no longer—in which the divine essence is communicated to you. This is ecstasy. It is the liberation of your mind from its finite consciousness. Like only can apprehend like; when you thus cease to be finite, you become one with the infinite. In the reduction of your soul to its simplest self, its divine essence, you realize this union—this identity."
–Plotinus

"Since beginning-less time, this mind has never been generated and has never been extinguished, is neither blue nor yellow, is without shape and without characteristic, does not belong to being and nonbeing, does not consider new or old, is neither long nor short, and is nether large nor small. It transcends all limitations, names, traces, and correlations. It in itself—that's it! To activate thoughts is to go against it! It is like space, which is boundless and immeasurable. It is only this one mind that is Buddha; there is no distinction between Buddhas and sentient beings. However, sentient beings are attached to characteristics and seek outside of themselves. Seeking it, they lose it even more. Sending the Buddha in search for the Buddha, grasping

the mind with the mind, they may exhaust themselves in striving for an entire eon but will never get it. They do not understand that if they cease their thoughts and end their thinking, the Buddha will automatically be present."
–Duanji, "Essentials of the Transmission of Mind," *Zen Texts,* trans. John R. McRae

"Become nothing, and He'll turn you into everything."
–Rumi, trans. Coleman Barks

"One cannot surrender completely to anything but God. … In the act of surrender there can be no forcing. Willing a release makes the release tighter because it does not yield to will. It yields to yielding. … By the act of surrender you realize the absolute control you have over your life. Surrender is a choice—an absolute personal choice. … Surrender can be proclaimed as the most selfish act because it leads to total fulfillment. … The final lesson for each soul is the total surrender to the will of God manifested in your own heart."
–Emmanuel's Book: A Manual for Living Comfortably in the Cosmos

"It is not danger that comes when defenses are laid down. It is safety. It is peace. It is joy. And it is God."
–*A Course in Miracles*, M-4.VI.11-15.

"This divine energy of Mine, consisting of the three modes of material nature, is difficult to overcome. But those who have surrendered unto Me can easily cross beyond it."
–Krishna, *Bhagavad-Gita, As it is,* trans. A.C. Bhaktivedanta Swami Prabhupada

"'Thou shalt love the lord, thy God, with all thy heart, with all thy soul, with all thy strength, and with all thy mind.' Think! Does the meaning come? Heart, soul, strength, mind. Is there anything to do at this point but to turn it all over to God, the Holy Spirit, the whole-I-spirit in action?"

–Baird T. Spalding, *Life and Teaching of the Masters of the Far East V.1*

"O scion of Bharata, surrender unto Him utterly. By His grace you will attain transcendental peace and the supreme and eternal abode."
–Krishna, *Bhagavad-Gita, As it is*, trans. A.C. Bhaktivedanta Swami Prabhupada

"Always think of Me, become My devotee, worship Me and offer your homage unto Me. Thus you will come to Me without fail. I promise you this because you are My very dear friend. … Abandon all varieties of religion and just surrender unto Me. I shall deliver you from all sinful reactions. Do not fear."
–Krishna, *Bhagavad-Gita, As it is*, trans. A.C. Bhaktivedanta Swami Prabhupada

"It is in thee, and if thou canst for a while cease from thinking and willing, thou shalt hear unspeakable words of God. When thou standest still from the thinking and willing of self, the eternal hearing, seeing and speaking will be revealed to thee, and so God heareth and seeth through thee."
–Jacob Behmen, as quoted in *Cosmic Consciousness* by Richard M Bucke

"The big lesson in Buddhism, then, the sense of what we have been saying is, 'Get away from your rational system and get into the wonderful experience that is moving through all things all the time.'"
–Joseph Campbell, *Reflections on the Art of Living*

"To be fully realized as the True Self, the Divine as what you are, requires one thing—to surrender to what you have always been at the cost of the known."
–Paul Selig, *The Book of Freedom*

7: Silence: the Truth is Beyond Logic and Language

"Silence is the language of God. All else is poor translation."
–Rumi, trans. Coleman Barks

To reach silence, surrender the intellect's and logic's need for language in order to understand. Words can never truly describe these heart openings, these eye openings, or any spiritual experience at all for that matter. One must experience it for themselves, and to experience it, one must let go of thoughts that are language based and of the intellect. Again, it is about moving into the heart. When you walk into a church, a temple, a holy place, a sacred space, you are quiet. Let it be so with the heart. It is the true residing place of our Creator. Be still, become silent, and listen.

The goal of most spiritual practices is to allow the individual to be more receptive. This is what becoming silent is all about. In order to receive the wisdom and love that is within, we must become still and give a silent space for it. Meditation is a tool for this. It allows us to become aware of the inner commentary and let it go. Only when we are silent do we receive the subtler perceptions of the subtler energies that we truly are.

"Look! Even now the King is raining treasure from the palace.
But this gold is caught only by those who make an empty space before it."
–Rumi, trans. Coleman Barks

"For God to make love, for the divine alchemy to work, the Pitcher needs a still cup. Why ask Hafiz to say anything more about your most vital requirement?"
–Hafiz, *The Gift*, trans. Daniel Ladinsky

"He who knows does not speak. He who speaks does not know. One must close one's mouth and close one's gates, blunt one's sharp wit, dissolve one's confused thoughts…"
–Lao-Tzu, *Tao-te Ching*, trans. Richard Wilhelm

"It is conceived of by him by whom It is not conceived of. He by whom It is conceived of, knows It not. It is not understood by those who [say they] understand It. It is understood by those who [say they] understand It not."
–Kena Upanishad 2.3-5, *The Thirteen Principal Upanishads* trans. Robert Ernest Hume

"The fool doth think he is wise, but the wise man knows himself to be a fool."
–William Shakespeare

"That which one thinks not with thought (manas, mind), that with which they say thought (manas, mind) is thought— That indeed know as Brahma, Not this that people worship as this. That which one sees not with sight, that with which one sees sights— That indeed know as Brahma, Not this that people worship as this."
–Kena Upanishad 1.4-5, *The Thirteen Principal Upanishads* trans. Robert Ernest Hume

"Let yourself experience a world you do not know. Do not give definition, shape, form, or structure to your non knowing. Let the only thing that exists be the experience of self at this moment. From this place, no words are needed, none are adequate."

–*Emmanuel's Book II: The Choice for Love*[18]

"I need a mouth as wide as the sky to say the nature of a True person, language as large as longing."
–Rumi, trans. Coleman Barks

"He should not meditate upon many words, for that is a weariness of speech."
–Brhadaranyaka Upanishad 4.4.21, *The Thirteen Principal Upanishads* trans. Robert Ernest Hume

"Many words lead to quick exhaustion; better to maintain emptiness within."
– Lao-Tzu, *Tao-te Ching*, trans. Richard John Lynn

"I am through with everything but you. I am dying into your mystery, and dying, I am now no other than that mystery. … I try whispering perfection, but no sound comes. You are beyond description, beyond even reason to be. We are the fishes in your sea, we are your gestures and your pleasures. But O, my love, you are not approached by thoughts like these. Love is not approached by thought at all."
–Rumi, trans. Coleman Barks

"Though words are spoken to explain the Void, the Void as such can never be expressed. Though we say, 'The mind is a bright light,' it is beyond all words and symbols."
–*Six Yogas of Naropa & Teachings on Mahamudra*

"How can I describe You when You are beyond the mind, the body, and the senses?"
–Shiva Mahimna Stotram

---

[18] Excerpt(s) from EMMANUEL'S BOOK II: THE CHOICE FOR LOVE compiled by Pat Rodegast and Judith Stanton, copyright © 1989 by Pat Rodegast. Used by permission of Bantam Books, an imprint of Random House, a division of Penguin Random House LLC. All rights reserved.

"The peace of God is shining in you now, and in all living things. In quietness is it acknowledged universally. For what your inward vision looks upon is your perception of the universe."
–*A Course in Miracles*, W-pI.188.5:5-7.

"And God Himself speaks to His Son, as His Son speaks to Him. Their language has no words, for what They say cannot be symbolized. Their knowledge is direct and wholly shared and wholly one."
–*A Course in Miracles,* W-pI.129.4:2-4.

"His peace surrounds you silently. God is very quiet."
–*A Course in Miracles*, T-11.III.1:5-6.

"The greater truth is beyond words. The greater truth liberates mind. The greater truth is simply the is-ness that is your Self."
–*Emmanuel's Book II: The Choice for Love*

"Our deepest feelings are precisely those we are least able to express, and even in the act of adoration, silence is our highest praise."
–Neville Goddard, *The Power of Awareness*

"We begin with the mental learn/teaching necessary for contact with intelligent infinity. The prerequisite of mental work is the ability to retain silence of self at a steady state when required by the self. The mind must be opened like a door. The key is silence."
–*The Law of One, Book 1*

"The supreme experience is staggering, enrapturing, blissful, and inspiring, but at the same time inexplicable and ungraspable by the intellect. The experience is supremely illuminating because it reveals the grandeur, sublimity and the eternal nature of the soul, but beyond that—what? All that is beyond lies out of the reach

of the intellect and hence cannot be translated into any language devised by the mind."
–Gopi Krishna, *Living with Kundalini: The autobiography of Gopi Krishna*

"Love lit a fire in my chest, and anything that wasn't love left: intellectual subtlety, philosophy, books, school… Love is a language that cannot be said or heard."
–Rumi, trans. Coleman Barks

8: Reality is a Dream we Create

> "Reality is created by the mind; we can change our reality by changing our mind."
> –Plato

> "All that we see or seem is but a dream within a dream."
> –Edgar Allan Poe

This truth has become popular and is most widely known as "the law of attraction," but I like to think of it as reality being a dream that we create. Why? Because like a dream, we tend to forget that we are dreaming and that we are the dreamer. We forget that we are co-creators and that we create our reality experience. We are so powerful as dream and reality creators that when we believe ourselves to be limited and separate, our reality reflects that and therefore reinforces that belief.

We become lost in our own creations.

I believe this is the point of the earth experience. To travel into the night is worth the experience of dawn. To intentionally forget the truth of our identity is well worth the rediscovery of it, because, oh what a glorious rediscovery it is! The transformation from the darkness into the light, the awakening back to what we really are, is a show the entire cosmos has gathered to watch.

Earth is an exciting place, where great dreamers come to dream, even at the risk of forgetting that they are dreaming.

How are we creating the dream? How do we create reality? We do so through our state of being. Our state of being is comprised of beliefs, thoughts, emotions and actions. We are an ultimate dream-creating machine. All aspects of our expression create reality. It starts with belief. With certain beliefs we generate corresponding thoughts, then emotions. Emotions are important. Like I mentioned before, they are energy in motion: e-motion. We then consequently act a certain way. The acting on it and embodying it is crucial. We must not keep it simply theoretical, but express it and live it, be it and feel it in our physical experience.

We are Creator; therefore, we constantly create reality. Reality is not separate from us but is an extension of us. It changes as we change, because it *is* us.

When we want to become something, change something, gain something, or attract something into our lives, we mustn't come from a place of wanting that which we are not or that which we don't have. This is putting yourself in a state of being of lack, and your state of being dictates your reality experience. As you are, so all shall be. Therefore, you will create more lack. Life is a mirror. To become or receive what you desire, behave, feel, and imagine you already are it or have it. Inundate yourself with the state of being of already achieving it. Then you will create it.

Sincere feelings and strong emotions are key. Become excited, passionate, stoked! The synchronicities will accelerate and be at first dizzying and mind-boggling. Then you will realize through your own direct experience the truth that you are a co-creator.

> "Humanity is a single being in spite of its many forms and faces, and there is in it only such seeming separation as we find in our own being when we are dreaming. The universe which we study with such care is a dream, and we the dreamers of the dream, eternal dreamers dreaming non-eternal dreams. One day, like Nebuchadnezzar, we shall awaken from the dream, from the nightmare in which we fought with demons, to find that we really never left our eternal home; that we were never born and have never died save in our dream."
>
> –Neville Goddard, *The Search (At Your Command)*

> "Awareness of dreaming is the real function of God's teachers. ... Unity alone is not a thing of dreams. And it is this God's

teachers acknowledge as behind the dream, beyond all seeming and yet surely theirs."
–*A Course in Miracles*, M-12.6:6-11.

"Your lenses will clear and you will see nothing but Angels walking in the masquerade of their own adventure."
–*Emmanuel's Book III: What is an Angel doing here?*

"We are God dreaming that we are not God."
–Mary Carroll Nelson, *The Toltec Prophecies of Don Miguel Ruiz*

"Your life is the manifestation of your dream; it is an art. … The dream you are living is your creation. It is your perception of reality that you can change at any time. You have the power to create hell, and you have the power to create heaven. Why not dream a different dream? Why not use your mind, your imagination, and your emotions to dream heaven?"
–Don Miguel Ruiz, *The Four Agreements*[19]

"According to your faith, be it unto you. All things are possible to them that believe."
–Jesus, Gospel of Thomas, *The Nag Hammadi Library*

"For as he thinketh in his heart, so is he."
–Proverbs 23:7, *The Holy Bible King James Version*

"A man consists of his faith, and as his faith is, so is he."
–Krishna, *Bhagavad-Gita*, trans. Barbara Stoler Miller

"Our life is shaped by our minds; we become what we think. Joy follows a pure thought like a shadow that never leaves."

---

[19] *The Four Agreements* © 1997 by don Miguel Ruiz and Janet Mills. Reprinted by permission of Amber-Allen Publishing, San Rafael, California. www.thefouragreements.com

–Gautama Buddha, *The Dhummapada*, trans. Eknath Easwaran[20]

"For whatever a man soweth, that shall he also reap."
–Galatians 6:7, *The Holy Bible King James Version*

"You will see it without *because* you saw it first within."
–*A Course in Miracles*, T-12.VII.12:3.

"Nothing is either good or bad but thinking makes it so."
–William Shakespeare, *Hamlet*, Act 2 Scene 2

"Every thought therefore is a cause and every condition is an effect; for this reason it is absolutely essential that you control your thoughts so as to bring forth only desirable conditions. … The world within is the cause, the world without is the effect; to change the effect you must change the cause."
–Charles Haanel, *The Master Key System*

"The world, and all within it, is man's conditioned consciousness objectified. Consciousness is the cause as well as the substance of the entire world. So it is to consciousness that we must turn if we would discover the secret of creation."
–Neville Goddard, *Feeling is the Secret*

"Your world is formulated by the consciousness of everyone on it."
–*Emmanuel's Book II: The Choice for Love*

"Thus, the mind creates the individual's world. … In this way the world is not the outside world, but the world with which one mentally associates."
–Harish Johari, *Chakras*

---

[20] From The Dhammapada, translated by Eknath Easwaran, founder of the Blue Mountain Center of Meditation, copyright 1985, 2007; reprinted by permission of Nilgiri Press, P. O. Box 256, Tomales, CA 94971, www.easwaran.org.

"The time has arrived, when all must understand, that thought and feeling are the only and mightiest creative power in Life or in the Universe."
–Godfre Ray King, *The I AM Discourses*

"Whatsoever things ye desire, when ye pray believe that you have received them, and ye shall have them."
–Mark 11:24, *The Holy Bible The King James Version*

"Nothing stops you from realizing your objective save your failure to feel that you are already that which you wish to be, or that you are already in possession of the thing sought."
–Neville Goddard, *Feeling is the Secret*

"According to your faith be it done to you."
–Matthew 9:29, *The Holy Bible English Standard Version*

"For to the one who has, more will be given, and he will have an abundance, but from the one who has not, even what he has will be taken away…"
–Matthew 13:12, *The Holy Bible English Standard Version*

"Now the fabric of reality that you share is malleable to thought, and this is what you don't understand. How you perceive anything informs the object of your perception."
–Paul Selig, *The Book of Freedom*

9: The One in Everything is Love

> "There is nothing but love. Don't let the masks and postures fool you."
> –*Emmanuel's Book: A Manual for Living Comfortably in the Cosmos*

Build love build

build love build
and each layer mend
until nothing else but you
and all else I do not comprehend

build love build
let me be still
and with childlike simplicity
surrender to your will

build love build
make my heart a fiery sun
open wide my forehead eye
let me see us as one

build love build
make my head a humming hive
thrill my body with your buzz
sweetest nectar come alive

build love build
reinstate innocence
and in every other being
let me see your presence

build love build
remind the mind of the eye
the key point of the universe
within is where it lies

build love build
and each layer mend
until nothing else but you
and all else I do not comprehend

We have come to the last truth, but most certainly not the least. It is by far the most important of them all. Without it, the rest are meaningless.

It is the ultimate lesson from Spirit: everything is love. The earth is love, the One is love, Spirit is love, consciousness is love, energy is love, you are love… God is love.

The crying during my openings was not from sorrow, but from an overwhelming love. A love arose within me that I can't possibly describe. So powerful was its force, I melted.

Under the ecstasy of divine, unlimited love all I could do was cry. There was no making any sense of it logically. All the mental noise of analysis, questioning, and judgment was hushed. The holy presence of potent love brought peace and silent awe.

This ineffable sensation of pure love-energy goes hand in hand with the previously explored attributes. All have at their core the feeling of being fully loved by the universe.

To remember, to reach enlightenment, and to feel this love, we shall love as Creator loves: everything unconditionally. The will of the One is to acknowledge and love the One in everything. It's that simple.

"This Supreme Lord who pervades all existence, the true self of all creatures, may be realized through undivided love."
–Krishna, *The Bhagavad-Gita*, trans. Eknath Easwaran

"When this great love is kindled in thee, it will burn as no fire can do... This fire of the love of God is brighter than the sun, sweeter than all besides, more supporting than all food and drink, and more to be desired than all the joys of this world."
–Jacob Boehme

"By love may He be gotten and holden, but by thought never."
–The Cloud of Unknowing

"I give you a new commandment, that you love one another. Just as I have loved you, you also should love one another."
–Jesus, John 13:34, *The New Oxford Annotated Bible*

"The message from the world of spirit can be stated with simplicity: Perfect love is all there is and perfect love must be experienced in the NOW. All else is fear's complexity."
–Emmanuel's Book II: The Choice for Love

"Just then a lawyer stood up to test Jesus. 'Teacher,' he said, 'what must I do to inherit eternal life?' He said to him, 'What is written in the law? What do you read there?' He answered, 'You shall love the Lord your God with all your heart, and with all your soul, and with all your strength, and with all your mind; and your neighbor as yourself.' And he said to him, 'You have given the right answer; do this, and you will live.'"
–Jesus, Luke 10:25-28, *The New Oxford Annotated Bible*

"Love one another, for God is love, and so shall his angels know that you walk in his paths."
–Jesus, *The Essene Gospel of Peace*

"When you say from the heart, 'I choose to know God's will,' then that is the fundamental use of free will. It is only with freedom of choice that this can take place. … When man's will is aligned with God's will it is an effortless existence in which the wisdom is in a place of comfort and loosely held control. To know the presence of God's will you need to listen to the many voices that live in you. You will find voices of fear, rage, contradiction, obstinacy, illusions of all sorts. When those voices become familiar, then the gentleness, the softness, warmth and Light of your inner wisdom can the more easily be heard. It contrasts with the cacophony of those other voices that are superimposed upon the inner knowing that is God's will."
–Emmanuel's Book: A Manual for Living Comfortably in the Cosmos

"To be willing that God express perfectly through us the highest ideal He has conceived is the meaning of, 'Not my will, but Thine, O God, be done.' None can rise above mortal thoughts without doing the will of God whether he does it consciously or unconsciously."
–Baird T. Spalding, *Life and Teaching of the Masters of the Far East V. 1*

"Love is not an activity of the mind, but is the 'Pure and Luminous Essence' which creates mind. This Essence from the Great God Flame streams into substance, and constantly pours itself out, as Perfection in form and action. Love is Perfection manifest. It can only express peace, joy, and an outpouring of those feelings to all creation unconditionally. It asks nothing for Itself because It is Eternally Self-Creating, being the Heartbeat of the 'Supreme.' Love owns All and is only concerned with setting the Plan of Perfection into action in all. Thus, It is a constant pouring out of Itself. It takes no cognizance of what has been given in the past, but receives Its joy and maintains Its balance by the continual Out-streaming of Itself. Because this Perfection is within Love, forever flowing forth, it is incapable of recording anything but Itself. Love alone is the basis of

harmony and the right use of all Life energy. In human experience, this grows into a desire to give, and give, and give of all the individual's peace and harmony unto the rest of creation."
–Godfre Ray King, *Unveiled Mysteries*

"The continual Outpouring of a Feeling of Peace and Divine Love to every person and everything unconditionally, no matter whether you think it be deserved or not, is the Magic Key that unlocks the door and releases instantly this 'Tremendous Inner God-Power.' Fortunate indeed is he who has learned this 'Law' for he then seeks to BE All Peace and Love. Without It humanity has nothing good, and with It they have all things 'Perfect.'"
–Godfre Ray King, *Unveiled Mysteries*

"God is love, and he who dwelleth in love dwelleth in God, and God in him."
–Jesus, John 4:16, *The Holy Bible King James Version*

"He that loveth not knoweth not God, for God is love."
–Jesus, John 4:8, *The Holy Bible King James Version*

"There is only one mighty, invisible, evolving, process, and that is through the power of consciously generating love. Love, being the hub of all life, the more we enter it, and use it consciously, the more easily and quickly we release this Mighty Power of God, that is always standing as a dammed-up force, waiting to find an opening in our own consciousness by which it can project itself."
–Godfre Ray King, *The I AM Discourses*

"Once the student becomes really aware that, 'God is Love,' and Love's True Activity comes through the heart, he will understand that to focus his attention on the desire to project Love forth, for any given purpose, is the supreme privilege of

the outer activity of the consciousness, which can generate Love to a boundless degree."
–Godfre Ray King, *The I AM Discourses*

"Whenever you are not wholly joyous, it is because you have reacted with a lack of love to one of God's creations."
–*A Course in Miracles,* T-5.VII.5:1.

"Love is your safety. Fear does not exist. Identify with love and you are safe. Identify with love and you are home. Identify with love and find your Self."
–*A Course in Miracles,* W-pII.5.5:5-8.

"Love is all that exists. Love is the universal communication. It is the energy that has created the universe and is keeping it going. God is love."
–*Emmanuel's Book: A Manual for Living Comfortably in the Cosmos*

"For I should not have known how to love the Lord, if He had not loved me. For who is able to distinguish love, except the one that is loved? … I have united to Him. For the lover has found the Beloved. And because I shall love Him that is the son, I shall become a son. For he that is joined to Him that is immortal, will also himself become immortal. And he who has pleasure in the living one, will become living."
–Odes of Solomon, Ode 3, *The Lost Books of the Bible and the forgotten books of Eden*

"Love has been defined by those who perceive its true character as the greatest thing in the world. I might add that it is the greatest healing force in the world. Love never fails to meet every demand of the human heart. The Divine Principle of Love may be used to eliminate every sorrow, every infirmity, every harsh condition, and every lack that harasses humanity."
–Baird T. Spalding, *Life and Teaching of the Masters of the Far East V.1*

"Love is the mother, we are her sons. She shines inside us, visible—invisible, as we trust or lose trust or feel it start to grow again."
–Rumi, *Birdsong*, trans. Coleman Barks

"Love the Lord thy God with all thy heart, with all thy soul, and with all thy strength: this is the first and greatest commandment. And the second is like unto it: Love thy neighbor as thyself. There is none other commandment greater than these."
–Jesus, *The Essene Gospel of Peace*

"The will to be served turns the life current against self. The will to serve keeps the life current flowing through self and keeps the self in radiation. To serve gives purpose to vision; it releases love in life. How can love be expressed unless it flows through the one expressing life? If it flows through the consciousness, the whole organism responds; it thrills every cell with the love it expresses. … The I AM is expressed through the me and the me is no longer allowed to suppress the I AM. … In no way can it be given higher expression than when it is allowed to fill the need of others. It is the flowing forth to others that opens the storehouse of Spirit. It is the 'I will to serve' that opens the unlimited storehouse of God to all and brings its realization to the soul."
–Baird T. Spalding, *Life and Teaching of the Masters of the Far East V.1*

"The good news, which the World Redeemer brings and which so many have been glad to hear, zealous to preach, but reluctant, apparently, to demonstrate, is that God is love, that He can be, and is to be, loved, and that all without exception are his children."
–Joseph Campbell, *The Hero with a Thousand Faces*

"Your intuitive heart is the doorway that stands between the worlds. In your willingness to go against all reason, all defenses, all habits, all patterns, all superstitions, and many teachings to say, 'I will love' you walk in the Light."
–*Emmanuel's Book II: The Choice for Love*

"There is no bond that can unite the divided but love: all else is a curse."
–Aleister Crowley, *The Book of the Law*

"But to love me is better than all things… invoking me with a pure heart, and the serpent flame therein, thou shalt come alittle to lie in my bosom… Put on the wings and arouse the coiled splendor within you: come unto me!"
–Aleister Crowley, *The Book of the Law*

"Love requires no practice. Love is. One cannot practice is-ness. One can, however, practice the decision to love. The path to love is found by experiencing what it is like without love just as the path to Light is to be aware of darkness. You make the supreme choice. Love is not mastered. It is allowed."
–*Emmanuel's Book: A Manual for Living Comfortably in the Cosmos*

"The best way of service to others is the constant attempt to seek to share the love of the Creator as it is known to the inner self. This involves self-knowledge and the ability to open the self to the other-self without hesitation. This involves, shall we say, radiating that which is the essence or the heart of the mind/body/spirit complex."
–*The Law of One, Book 1*

"The root cause of blockage is the lack of the ability to see the other-self as the Creator, or to phrase this differently, the lack of love."
–*The Law of One, Book 4*

"You can witness someone in their perfection and transform their consciousness. You can see yourself as perfect and transform your own... You are love incarnate when you love."
–Paul Selig, *I Am the Word*

"...the easiest way to understand is that what you are, in recognition of your world, will make no claim upon another but one that is in love. You are the emissary of the vibration of love, and the claim you make for another will be in agreement to this."
–Paul Selig, *The Book of Freedom*

Contact

contact@theeyeopening.com
www.theeyeopening.com
Instagram: @theeyeopening

Sources & Permissions

The Bhagavad-Gita. Trans. Eknath Easwaran. Berkeley: Blue Mountain Center of Meditation, 1985.
From The Bhagavad Gita, translated by Eknath Easwaran, founder of the Blue Mountain Center of Meditation, copyright 1985, 2007; reprinted by permission of Nilgiri Press, P. O. Box 256, Tomales, CA 94971, www.easwaran.org.

Bhagavad-Gita, As it is. Trans. A.C. Bhaktivedanta Swami Prabhupada. 2nd ed. Singapore: Bhaktivedanta's Book Trust International, Inc., 1989.
Text courtesy of the Bhaktivedanta Book Trust International, Inc. www.Krishna.com. Used with permission

The Bhagavad-Gita: Krishna's Counsel in Time of War. Trans. Barbara Stoler Miller. New York: Bantam Books, 2004. pp. 66, 98, 118, 137.
Excerpt(s) from THE BHAGAVAD-GITA: KRISHNA'S COUNSEL IN TIME OF WAR by Barbara Miller, translation copyright © 1986 by Barbara Stoler Miller. Used by permission of Bantam Books, an imprint of Random House, a division of Penguin Random House LLC. All rights reserved.

Blake, William. *The Complete Poetry & Prose of William Blake.* Ed. David V. Erdman. New York: Anchor Books, 1982.

Blavatsky, H.P.. *The Secret Doctrine.* Vol. 1. California: Theosophical University Press, 1886.

Bonnie Turner, et al. "The Ego Virtue Of Fidelity As A Psychosocial Rite Of Passage In The Transition From Adolescence To Adulthood." *Child & Youth Care Forum* 27.5 (1998): 337-354. *Academic Search Premier.* Web. 16 Nov. 2012.

Bucke, Richard M. *Cosmic Consciousness.* New York: University Books Inc., 1961.

Campbell, Joseph. *The Hero with a Thousand Faces.* Novato, CA: New World Library, 2008. pp. 30-31, 135.
From Joseph Campbell's *The Hero with a Thousand Faces* Copyright © Joseph Campbell Foundation (jcf.org) 2008. Used with permission.

____. *The Inner Reaches of Outer Space.* Novato, California: New World Library, 2002. p. 36.
From Joseph Campbell's *The Inner Reaches of Outer Space* Copyright © Joseph Campbell Foundation (jcf.org) 2002. Used with permission.

____. *The Masks of God: Primitive Mythology.* New York: Penguin Books Arkana, 1991. p. 88.

____. *The Mythic Image.* Princeton University Press, 1981. p. 331.

____. *Myths to Live By.* New York: Penguin Books Arkana, 1993. p. 230.

____. *Pathways to Bliss.* Novato, CA: New World Library, 2004. p. 11.

____. *Reflections on the Art of Living, A Joseph Campbell Companion.* Ed. Diane K. Osbon. New York: Harper Perennial, 1991. pp. 107, 109, 146, 206.
From Joseph Campbell's *Reflections on the Art of Living, A Joseph Campbell Companion* Copyright © Joseph Campbell Foundation (jcf.org) 1991. Used with permission.

Crowley, Aleister. *The Book of the Law.* San Francisco: Weiser Books, Red wheel / Weiser, 1976. Pp. 23, 27, 29.

Danaos, Kosta. *The Magus of Java.* Vermont: Inner Traditions, 2000. p. 50. *The Magus of Java* by Kosta Danaos published by Inner Traditions International and Bear & Company, ©2000. All rights reserved. http://www.Innertraditions.com Reprinted with permission of publisher.

The Dhammapada. Trans. Eknath Easwaran. Berkeley: Blue Mountain Center of Meditation, 1985.
From The Dhammapada, translated by Eknath Easwaran, founder of the Blue Mountain Center of Meditation, copyright 1985, 2007; reprinted by permission of Nilgiri Press, P. O. Box 256, Tomales, CA 94971, www.easwaran.org.

The Essene Gospel of Peace. Trans. Edmond Bordeaux Szekely. San Diego: Academy of Creative Living, 1970.

Frissell, Bob. *You are a Spiritual Being Having a Human Experience.* Berkeley: North Atlantic Books, 2001. p. 90.
From *You Are a Spiritual Being Having a Human Experience* by Bob Frissell published by Frog Books/North Atlantic Books, copyright © 2001 by Bob Frissell. Reprinted by permission of North Atlantic Books.

Goddard, Neville. *At Your Command.* 7 September 2015. http://www.atyourcommand.org/

____. *Feeling is the Secret.* 7 September 2015. http://www.feelingisthesecret.org/

____. *The Power of Awareness.* 7 September 2015. http://www.thepowerofawareness.org/

Grof, Stanislav. "Frontiers of the Mind." *healthy.net,* 7 Jan. 2019. healthy.net/Health/Interview/Frontiers_of_the_Mind/200

Grof, Stanislov and Christina, editors. *Spiritual Emergency: When Personal Transformaion Becomes a Crisis.* Los Angeles: Tarcher, 1989.

Haanel, Charles F. *The Master Key System.* New York: Barnes and Noble Inc., 2007. p. 7.

Hafiz. *The Gift.* Trans. Daniel Ladinsky. New York: Penguin Compass, 1999.

Hall, Manly P.. *The Secret Teachings of All Ages.* New York: Putnam Tarcher, 2003. pp. 99, 272.

The Holy Bible, King James Version. New York: American Bible Society: 1999; Bartleby.com, 2000. www.bartleby.com/108/.

Huxley, Aldous. *The Perennial Philosophy.* London: Chatto & Windus, 1969.

International Religious Foundation. *World Scripture: A Comparative Anthology of Sacred Texts.* Ed. Wilson, Andrew. St. Paul: Paragon House, 1991.

Jennings, Hargrave. *Ophiolatreia.* Privately Printed, 1889.

Johari, Harish. *Chakras* by Harish Johari published by Inner Traditions International and Bear & Company, ©2000. All rights reserved. http://www.Innertraditions.com Reprinted with permission of publisher. p. 64.

Jung, C. G. *The Psychology of Kundalini Yoga.* ed. Sonu Shamdasani. Princeton, New Jersey: Princeton University Press, 1996. pp. xxv, 57, 89, 106.

King, Godfre Ray. *The I AM Discourses by the Ascended Master Saint Germain.* Vol.3 2nd ed. Chicago: Saint Germain Press, 1936. pp. 35, 60, 89, 115, 120.

____. *Unveiled Mysteries.* Chicago: Saint Germain Press, 1934. pp. 58-59, 234, 236, 257.

Krishna, Gopi. *The Awakening of Kundalini.* Markdale, ON Canada: The Institute for Consciousness Research. Amazon KDP Edition ,ebook.

_____. *Living with Kundalini, Autobiography of Gopi Krishna.* Boston: Shambhala Publications, Inc., 1993. pp. 122, 144-145, 155, 252, 267, 340, 385. From *Living with Kundalini: The Autobiography of Gopi Krishna*, by Gopi Krishna, © 1967, 1970 by James Hillman. Reprinted by arrangement with The Permissions Company, LLC, on behalf of Shambhala Publications, Inc., Boulder, Colorado, https://www.shambhala.com/

_____. *Kundalini: The Secret of Yoga.* Markdale, ON Canada: The Institute for Consciousness Research. Amazon KDP Edition, ebook. p. 3159.

Lao-Tzu. *The Classic of the Way and Virtue: A New Translation of the Tao-te Ching of Laozi as Interpreted by Wang Bi.* Trans. Robert John Lynn. New York: Columbia University Press, 1999.

_____. *Tao Te Ching.* Trans. Richard Wilhelm. London: Penguin Arkana, 1985.

The Lost Books of the Bible and the forgotten books of Eden. Cleveland: The World Publishing Company, Alpha House Inc., 1926.

McCarty, James Allen, and Carla Rueckert, and Don Elkins. *The Law of One: The Ra Material.* Books 1-4. Louisville, KY: L/L Research, 1984. Apple iBooks. Book 1: pp. 190, 194, 294, 370. Book 2: p. 248. Book 3: p. 337. Book 4: p. 224. Free copy online: LLResearch.org

McRae, John R.. "Essentials of the Transmission of Mind." *Zen Texts.* Berkeley: Numata Center for Buddhists Translation and Research, 2005. Bukkyo Dendo Kyokai America, Inc.

Moses, Jeffery. *Oneness.* New York: Fawcett Columbine Books, 1989.

The Nag Hammadi Library in English. Ed. James M. Robinson. Boston: Brill, 1997.

Nelson, Mary Carroll. *The Toltec Prophecies of Don Miguel Ruiz.* Tusla, OK: Council Oak Books, 2003.

The New Oxford Annotated Bible. Ed. Michael D. Coogan. New York: Oxford University Press, 2001.

Rodegast, Pat, and Judith Stanton. *Emmanuel's Book: A Manual for Living Comfortably in the Cosmos.* New York: Bantam Books, 1985. pp. 7, 31-35, 47-49.
Excerpt(s) from EMMANUEL'S BOOK: A MANUAL FOR LIVING COMFORTABLY IN THE COSMOS compiled by Pat Rodegast and Judith Stanton, copyright © 1985 by Pat Rodegast. Used by permission of Bantam Books, an imprint of Random House, a division of Penguin Random House LLC. All rights reserved.

____. *Emmanuel's Book II: The Choice for Love.* New York: Bantam Books, 1989. pp. 20, 41, 44, 94, 219.
Excerpt(s) from EMMANUEL'S BOOK II: THE CHOICE FOR LOVE compiled by Pat Rodegast and Judith Stanton, copyright © 1989 by Pat Rodegast. Used by permission of Bantam Books, an imprint of Random House, a division of Penguin Random House LLC. All rights reserved.

____. *Emmanuel's Book III: What is an Angel doing here?* New York: Bantam Books, 1994. pp. 20, 110, 149, 221.
Excerpt(s) from EMMANUEL'S BOOK III: WHAT IS AN ANGEL DOING HERE? compiled by by Pat Rodegast and Judith Stanton, copyright © 1994 by Pat Rodegast and Judith Stanton. Used by permission of Bantam Books, an imprint of Random House, a division of Penguin Random House LLC. All rights reserved.

Ruiz, Don Miguel. *The Four Agreements.* San Rafael, CA: Amber-Allen Publishing, 2001.

The Four Agreements © 1997 by don Miguel Ruiz and Janet Mills. Reprinted by permission of Amber-Allen Publishing, San Rafael, California. All rights reserved. www.thefouragreements.com

Rumi. *Bird Song, Rumi.* Trans. Coleman Barks. Athens, GA: Maypop, 1993.

_____. *A New Illuminated Rumi, One Song.* Ed. Michael Green. Trans. Coleman Barks. Philadelphia: Running Press, 2005.

Sacred Books of the East. Ed. F. Max Mueller. "Buddist Mahayana Texts: Vajracchedika (The Diamond Cutter)", Part II. Vol. 49. Trans. F. Max Mueller, E.B. Cowell, J. Takakusu. Oxford: The Clarendon Press, 1894.

_____. "Qur'an", Part I, II. Vol. 6 of 48. Trans. E.H. Palmer. Oxford: The Clarendon Press, 1885

Schucman, Helen, and William Thetford. *A Course in Miracles.* New York: Foundation for Inner Peace, 1975.
All quotes are from *A Course in Miracles*, copyright ©1992, 1999, 2007 by the Foundation for Inner Peace, P.O. Box 598, Mill Valley, CA 94942-0589, www.acim.org and info@acim.org, used with permission.

Selig, Paul. *I Am the Word.* New York: Jeremy P. Tarcher / Penguin, 2010. pp. 20, 244, 294. Excerpt(s) from I AM THE WORD: A GUIDE TO THE CONSCIOUSNESS OF MAN'S SELF IN A TRANSITIONING TIME by Paul Selig, copyright © 2010 by Paul Selig. Used by permission of TarcherPerigee, an imprint of the Penguin Publishing Group, a division of Penguin Random House LLC . All rights reserved.

_____. *The Book of Freedom.* New York: Jeremy P. Tarcher / Penguin, 2018. pp. xx, 43, 176, 187, 310.
Excerpt(s) from THE BOOK OF FREEDOM by Paul Selig, copyright © 2018 by Paul Selig. Used by permission of Tarcher, an

imprint of Penguin Publishing Group, a division of Penguin Random House LLC. All rights reserved.

____. *The Book of Mastery*. New York: Jeremy P. Tarcher / Penguin, 2016. Audiobook, T3 42:00, T5 20:30.
Excerpt(s) from THE BOOK OF MASTERY: THE MASTERY TRILOGY: BOOK I by Paul Selig, copyright © 2016 by Paul Selig. Used by permission of TarcherPerigee, an imprint of the Penguin Publishing Group, a division of Penguin Random House LLC . All rights reserved.

____. *The Book of Truth*. New York: Jeremy P. Tarcher / Penguin, 2017. pp. 69, 184, 289.
Excerpt(s) from THE BOOK OF TRUTH: THE MASTERY TRILOGY: BOOK II by Paul Selig, copyright © 2017 by Paul Selig. Used by permission of TarcherPerigee, an imprint of the Penguin Publishing Group, a division of Penguin Random House LLC . All rights reserved.

The Six Yogas of Naropa & Teachings on Mahamudra. Trans. Garma C.C. Chang. Ithaca, NY: Snow Lion Publications, 1963.

Spalding, Baird T. *Life and Teaching of the Masters of the Far East*. 4 vols. Marina del Rey: Devross, 1924. V.1: pp. 12, 23, 30-31, 47, 50, 118, 139. V.3: p. 51.

Sullwold, Edith. "Swimming With Seals: The Developmental Role Of Initiation Rituals In Work With Adolescents." *Child & Youth Care Forum* 27.5 (1998): 305-315. *Academic Search Premier*. Web. 16 Nov. 2012.

Svoboda, Robert E. *Aghora II: Kundalini*. Las Vegas: Brotherhood of Life, 1993.

The Thirteen Principal Upanishads. trans. Robert Ernest Hume. Oxford University Press, 1921.
4/23/2019. <https://oll.libertyfund.org/titles/2058>

The Upanishads. Trans. Eknath Easwaran. Berkeley: Blue Mountain Center of Meditation, 1985.
From The Upanishads, translated by Eknath Easwaran, founder of the Blue Mountain Center of Meditation, copyright 1987, 2007; reprinted by permission of Nilgiri Press, P. O. Box 256, Tomales, Ca 94971, www.easwaran.org.

The Upanishads. Trans. Valerie J. Roebuck. New York: Penguin Classics, 2003.

Waters, Frank. *Book of the Hopi.* Princeton University Press, 1977. p. 33

Woodroffe, Sir John. *The Serpent Power.* India, Pondicherry: Ganesh & Co., 2006.

Made in the USA
Monee, IL
15 January 2021

57728586R00090